# special
# familyknits

# special familyknits

## 25 handknits for all seasons

### debbie bliss

COLLINS & BROWN

First published in the United Kingdom in 2007 by
Collins & Brown
151 Freston Road
London
W10 6TH

An imprint of Anova Books Company Ltd

Commissioning Editor: Michelle Lo
Editor: Kate Haxell
Photographer: Tim Young
Design Manager: Gemma Wilson
Designer: Louise Leffler
Illustrators: Luise Roberts and Stella Smith
Editorial Assistant: Katie Hudson
Senior Production Controller: Morna McPherson

ISBN 13: 978-1-843403-43-2

A CIP catalogue record for this book is available
from the British Library.

10 9 8 7 6 5 4 3 2 1

Reproduction by Anorax
Printed and bound by SNP Leefung, China

This book can be ordered direct from the
publisher. Contact the marketing department, but
try your bookshop first.

www.anovabooks.com

# CONTENTS

# INTRODUCTION

The collection of designs in *Special Family Knits* has given me the opportunity to indulge my love of stitch and style. Cables and bobbles, ribs and Fair Isle – all my favourite classic stitch patterns are here, but worked in contemporary shapes for a flattering fit.

New knitters are often attracted to the craft by easy patterns that use the wonderful array of fancy yarns now available. They can produce fabulous textures without needing to know more than simple knit and purl. However, as every knitter knows, once you have taken that first step, and then see the endless possibilities that the craft offers, you cannot wait to start the journey that takes you into creating knitted textures through combining stitches and colour.

With this in mind when designing the 25 pieces featured in this book, I wanted to show how the knitted fabric can work to create a look; a simple ribbed yoke on a child's summer coat pulls in to give a sweet, A-line effect, or the waist of a cardigan is defined by cables. I have also tried to vary the styles so that there is something to choose whatever your shape or size. There is a luxurious, cabled coat, casual cotton knits and relaxed summer tops. Accessories include an Aran bag, lacy, pure cashmere socks and a Fair Isle beanie. The collection covers a range of knitting skills from the basic to the more experienced, and for women, where the pattern allows for it, they are graded up to larger sizes.

The yarns I have used from my ranges have also been specifically chosen to work with the individual styles. Soft, cashmere mix yarns allow some garments to drape beautifully, while crisp cottons enhance the stitch detail on others. The colour palettes reflect the feel of the different styles: pale duck-egg blue, navy and white for the beach; warm earthy tones for the country; and apple green and raspberry for a summer picnic.

Lastly, nothing quite compares to the labour of love of knitting for the people in our lives, family or friends. A treasured handknit is a lasting reminder.

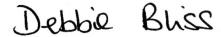

# BEACH

The cotton knits are inspired by the seascape, which is reflected in the palette of greyish blues, navy, and a chalky white. Guernseys and cables are enhanced by the crispness of the yarn.

# boat sweater

## MEASUREMENTS

To fit ages

| 2 | 4 | 6 years |
|---|---|---|

Finished measurements

Chest

| 72 | 82 | 90cm |
|---|---|---|

Length

| 35 | 38 | 42cm |
|---|---|---|

Sleeve length

| 22 | 25 | 28cm |
|---|---|---|

## MATERIALS

6(7:8) 50g balls of Debbie Bliss cotton dk
in White
Pair of each size 3.75mm and 4mm knitting
needles

## TENSION

20 sts and 30 rows to 10cm square over patt
when lightly pressed, using 4mm needles.

## ABBREVIATIONS

beg = beginning; cont = continue;
cm = centimetres; foll = following;
inc = increase; k = knit; p = purl; patt = pattern;
rem = remaining; rep = repeat; sl = slip;
st(s) = stitch(es); st st = stocking stitch.

## BACK

* With 4mm needles, cast on 72(82:90) sts.

**1st row** (right side) Purl.

**2nd row** Knit.

**3rd row** Purl.

**4th row** (wrong side) Purl.

**5th row** Knit.

**6th row** Purl.

These 6 rows form the reverse st st and st st
stripe patt and are repeated throughout. *
Cont until 100(108:120) rows from cast on edge
have been worked, so ending with a 4th(6th:6th)
row of 6-row stripe patt.

**\*\* Shape neck**

**Next row** (right side) Patt 23(26:29), turn and
cont on these sts only, leave rem sts on a
spare needle.
Dec 1 st at neck edge on next 4 rows.
Patt 1 row.
Cast off.
With right side facing, slip 26(30:32) sts at
centre back onto a holder, rejoin yarn to rem sts,
patt to end.
Dec 1 st at neck edge on next 4 rows.
Patt 1 row.
Cast off. \*\*

## FRONT

Work as Back from * to *.
Cont until 63(69:75) rows from cast on edge
have been worked, so ending with a right side
3rd row of 6-row stripe patt.

**Place chart**

**Next row** (wrong side) Patt 23(28:32), work

across 26 sts of 1st row of chart (reading chart from left to right), patt 23(28:32).

**Next row** (right side) Patt 23(28:32), work across 26 sts of 2nd row of chart, patt 23(28:32).

Cont in this way until all 27 chart rows have been worked, keeping 6-row stripe patt at each side correct.

Patt a further 10(12:18) rows, so ending with a 4th(6th:6th) row of 6-row stripe patt.

Now work as Back from ** to **.

### SLEEVES

With 4mm needles, cast on 36(38:40) sts.

Work in 6-row stripe patt as given for Back, **at the same time**, inc 1 st at each end of 5th row and every foll 6th(5th:5th) row until there are 54(66:70) sts.

Cont straight in patt until sleeve measures 22(25:28)cm from cast on edge, ending with a wrong side row.

Cast off.

### NECKBAND

Join right shoulder seam.

With right side facing and 3.75mm needles, pick up and k7 sts down left front neck, k(p:p) across 26(30:32) sts at centre front, pick up and k7 sts up right front neck and 7 sts down right back neck, k(p:p) across 26(30:32) sts at centre back, then pick up and k7 sts up left back neck 80(88:92) sts.

**Next row** (6th(2nd:2nd) patt row) P(k:k) to end.

Patt a further 8(12:12) rows, so ending with a wrong side row.

Cast off purlwise.

### TO MAKE UP

Press very lightly to slightly flatten the pattern.

Join left shoulder and neckband seam.

Matching centre of cast off edge of sleeve to shoulder, sew on sleeves. Join side and sleeve seams, carefully matching stripes.

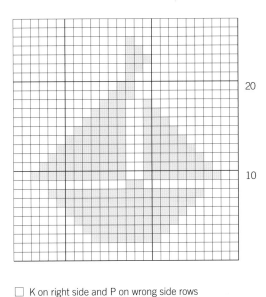

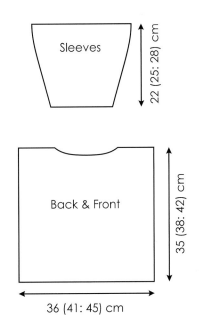

Sleeves

22 (25: 28) cm

Back & Front

35 (38: 42) cm

36 (41: 45) cm

20

10

☐ K on right side and P on wrong side rows
☐ P on right side and K on wrong side rows

# hooded guernsey

## MEASUREMENTS

To fit ages

| 1 | 2 | 3 | 4 years |
|---|---|---|---|

Finished measurements

Chest

| 67 | 71 | 77 | 83cm |
|---|---|---|---|

Length

| 30 | 36 | 42 | 48cm |
|---|---|---|---|

Sleeve length

| 19 | 22 | 25 | 28cm |
|---|---|---|---|

## MATERIALS

10(12:13:15) 50g balls of Debbie Bliss
cotton dk in Navy
Pair of each size 3.75mm and 4mm knitting
needles

## TENSION

20 sts and 28 rows to 10cm square over st st,
using 4mm needles.

## ABBREVIATIONS

beg = beginning; cm = centimetres;
cont = continue; dec = decrease;
foll = following; inc = increase; k = knit;
p = purl; patt = pattern; rem = remaining;
rep = repeat; skpo = sl 1, k1, pass slipped st
over; sl = slip; st(s) = stitch(es); st st = stocking
stitch; tog = together.

## BACK

With 3.75mm needles, cast on 69(73:79:85) sts.
Beg with a k row, work 2 rows in st st.
**Moss st row** K1, * p1, k1; rep from * to end.
Rep this row 5 times more.
Change to 4mm needles.
** Beg with a k row, work in st st until back
measures 15(19:23:27)cm from cast on edge,
ending with a p row.
**Next row** (right side) P to end.
**Next row** K to end.
**Shape armholes**
**Next row** Cast off 7(7:8:9) sts, k to end.
**Next row** Cast off 7(7:8:9) sts, p to end.
55(59:63:67) sts.
Now work in yoke patt as follows:
**Next row** (right side) P to end.
**Next row** K to end.
**Next row** K to end.
**Next row** K1, * p1, k1; rep from * to end.
Rep the last row 7 times more.
**Next row** P to end.
Rep the last 12 rows 3 times more.
**2nd, 3rd and 4th sizes only**
**Next row** P to end.
**Next row** K to end.
**Next row** K to end.
**Next row** P to end.
**3rd and 4th sizes only**
Rep the last 4 rows (1:2) times more.
**All sizes**
**Shape neck**
**Next row** (right side) P17(18:20:21), turn and
work on these sts for first side of neck shaping,

leave rem sts on a spare needle.
**Next row** K2tog, k to end.
**Next row** K to last 2 sts, k2tog.
**Next row** P2tog, p to end. 14(15:17:18) sts.
**Next row** P to end.
**Next row** K to end.
**Next row** K to end.
**Next row** P to end.
Cast off.
With right side facing, slip centre 21(23:23:25)
sts onto a holder, rejoin yarn to sts on spare
needle, p to end.
Complete to match first side.

## POCKET LINING

With 4mm needles, cast on 49(53:57:61) sts.
Beg with a k row, work in st st until pocket lining
measures 3(3:4:4)cm, ending with a p row.
Leave these sts on a spare needle

## FRONT

Work as given for Back until front measures
5(6:6:6)cm ending with a p row.
Break off yarn.
**Next row** (right side) Place first 10(10:11:12) sts
on a holder, attach yarn to next st, k1, skpo,
k43(47:51:55), k2tog, k1, turn and leave rem
10(10:11:12) sts on a holder.
Cont on centre 47(51:55:59) sts only.
**Next row** (wrong side) P.
**Next row** K1, skpo, k to last 3 sts, k2tog, k1.
Rep the last 2 rows 11(12:13:14) times more.
23(25:27:29) sts.

**Next row** P to end, leave these sts on a holder. Return to sts on holders.

With right side facing, k across first 10(10:11:12) sts, k49(53:57:61) sts of pocket lining, k rem 10(10:11:12) sts. 69(73:79:85) sts.

Beg with a p row work 25(27:29:31) rows in st st.

**Next row** (right side) K23(24:26:28), with sts of front in front of pocket lining sts, [k next st tog with next st from pocket lining] 23(25:27:29) times, k to end.

P 1 row.

Cont to work as given for Back from ** to end.

### SLEEVES

With 3.75mm needles, cast on 37(41:45:49) sts.

Beg with a k row, work 2 rows in st st.

**Moss st row** K1, * p1, k1; rep from * to end.

Rep this row 5 times more.

Change to 4mm needles.

Beg with a k row, work in st st and inc one st at each end of the 3rd(5th:3rd:3rd) row and every foll 4th row until there are 59(67:75:83) sts, ending with a p row.

Cont straight until sleeve measures 19(22:25:28)cm from cast on edge, ending with a wrong side row.

Place a marker at each end of last row.

Work a further 10(10:12:12) rows.

Cast off.

### NECKBAND

Join right shoulder seam.

With right side facing and 3.75mm needles, pick up and k8 sts down left front neck, k across 21(23:23:25) sts from front neck holder, pick up and k8 sts up right front neck, 8 sts down right back neck, k across 21(23:23:25) sts from back

neck, then pick up and k9 sts up left back neck. 75(79:79:83) sts.

**Moss st row** K1, * p1, k1; rep from * to end.

Rep this row 5 times more.

Cast off in moss st.

### HOOD

With 4mm needles, cast on 95(99:103:107) sts.

Beg with a k row, work in st st until hood measures 20(23:26:29)cm from cast on edge, ending with a p row.

**Next row** K1, * p1, k1; rep from * to end.

Rep the last row 5 times more.

Cast off in moss st.

### POCKET EDGINGS (both alike)

With right side facing and 3.75mm needles, pick up and k25(27:29:31) sts along edge of pocket opening.

**Next row** K1, * p1, k1; rep from * to end.

Rep the last row twice more.

Cast off in moss st.

### TO MAKE UP

Join left shoulder and neckband seam. Fold hood in half along cast on edge and join to form back seam. Sew hood to inside of neck edge. Sew sleeves into armholes with row ends above markers sewn to sts cast off at underarm. Join side and sleeve seams.

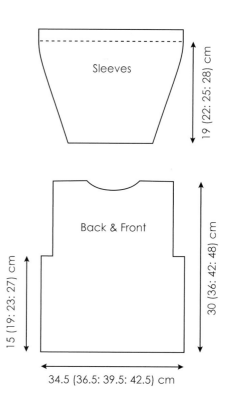

Sleeves

19 (22: 25: 28) cm

Back & Front

15 (19: 23: 27) cm

30 (36: 42: 48) cm

34.5 (36.5: 39.5: 42.5) cm

# baby jacket with ribbed sleeves

## MEASUREMENTS

To fit ages

3–6  6–9  9–12  12–18  18–24 months

Finished measurements

Chest

53  57  61  65  69cm

Length to shoulder

24  26  28  32  36cm

Sleeve length

13  15  17  20  22cm

## MATERIALS

4(5:5:6:7) 50g balls of Debbie Bliss cotton dk
in Lime

Pair of each size of 3.25mm and 4mm knitting
needles

20(20:25:25:30)cm open-ended zip

1 button

## TENSION

20 sts and 28 rows to 10cm square over st st
using 4mm needles.

## ABBREVIATIONS

alt = alternate; beg = beginning; cm =
centimetres; cont = continue; dec = decrease;
foll = following; inc = increase; k = knit;
p = purl; patt = pattern; rem = remaining;
rep = repeat; st(s) = stitch(es);
st st = stocking stitch; tog = together;
yrn = yarn round needle.

## BACK

With 3.25mm needles, cast on 54(58:62:66:70)
sts.

**1st, 3rd and 5th sizes only**

**1st row** (right side) K2, * p2, k2; rep from
* to end.

**2nd row** P2, * k2, p2; rep from * to end.

**2nd and 4th sizes only**

**1st row** (right side) P2, * k2, p2; rep from
* to end.

**2nd row** K2, * p2, k2; rep from * to end.

**All sizes**

Rep the last 2 rows 4 times more.

Change to 4mm needles.

Beg with a k row, work in st st until back
measures 14(15:16:19:22)cm from cast on
edge, ending with a p row.

**Shape armholes**

Cast off 4 sts at beg of next 2 rows.

46(50:54:58:62) sts.

Cont straight until back measures
24(26:28:32:36)cm from cast on edge, ending
with a wrong side row.

**Shape shoulders**

Cast off 11(13:14:16:17) sts at beg of next
2 rows.

Cast off rem 24(24:26:26:28) sts.

## LEFT FRONT

With 3.25mm needles, cast on 28(30:32:34:36)
sts.

**1st, 3rd and 5th sizes only**

**1st row** (right side) K2, * p2, k2; rep from
* to last 6 sts, p2, k4.

**2nd row** * K2, p2; rep from * to end.

**2nd and 4th sizes only**

**1st row** (right side) P2, * k2, p2; rep from * to
last 4 sts, k4.

**2nd row** K2, * p2, k2; rep from * to end.

**All sizes**

Rep the last 2 rows 4 times more.

Change to 4mm needles.

**1st row** (right side) Knit.

**2nd row** K2, p to end.

These 2 rows form st st with garter st border
and are repeated.

Cont until front measures 14(15:16:19:22)cm
from cast on edge, ending with a wrong
side row.

**Shape armhole**

Cast off 4 sts at beg of next row.

24(26:28:30:32) sts.

Cont straight until front measures
20(20:24:25:30)cm from cast on edge, ending
with a wrong side row.

**Shape neck**

**Next row** K to last 7(8:8:9:9) sts, leave these sts
on a holder.

Dec one st at neck edge on every row until
11(13:14:16:17) sts rem.

Cont straight until front measures same as Back
to shoulder, ending at armhole edge.

**Shape shoulder**

Cast off.

## RIGHT FRONT

With 3.25mm needles, cast on 28(30:32:34:36) sts.

**1st, 3rd and 5th sizes only**

**1st row** (right side) K4, * p2, k2; rep from * to end.

**2nd row** *P2, k2; rep from * to end.

**2nd and 4th sizes only**

**1st row** (right side) K4, p2, * k2, p2; rep from * to end.

**2nd row** K2, * p2, k2; rep from * to end.

**All sizes**

Rep the last 2 rows 4 times more.

Change to 4mm needles.

**1st row** (right side) Knit.

**2nd row** P to last 2 sts, k2.

These 2 rows form st st with garter st border and are repeated.

Cont until front measures 14(15:16:19:22)cm from cast on edge, ending with a right side row.

**Shape armhole**

Cast off 4 sts at beg of next row.

24(26:28:30:32) sts.

Cont straight until front measures 20(20:24:25:30)cm from cast on edge, ending with a wrong side row.

**Shape neck**

**Next row** (right side) K7(8:8:9:9), leave these sts on a holder, k to end.

Dec one st at neck edge on every row until 11(13:14:16:17) sts rem.

Cont straight until front measures same as Back to shoulder, ending at armhole edge.

**Shape shoulder**

Cast off.

## SLEEVES

With 3.25mm needles, cast on 34(34:34:38:38) sts.

**1st row** (right side) K2, * p2, k2; rep from * to end.

**2nd row** P2, * k2, p2; rep from * to end.

Rep the last 2 rows 4 times more.

Change to 4mm needles.

Cont in rib and inc one st at each end of the next(next:next:5th:5th) row and every foll alt row until there are 56(62:68:74:78) sts, taking all inc sts into rib.

Cont straight until sleeve measures 13(15:17:20:22)cm from cast on edge, ending with a wrong side row.

Mark each end of last row with a coloured thread.

Work a further 6 rows.

Cast off.

## POCKET

With 4mm needles, cast on 12(12:16:16:20) sts.

**1st row** (right side) K3, [p2, k2] 1(1:2:2:3) times, p2, k3.

**2nd row** P3, [k2, p2] 1(1:2:2:3) times, k2, p3.

Rep these 2 rows 5(5:6:6:7) times more.

**Buttonhole row** Rib 5(5:7:7:9), yrn, rib 2tog, rib to end.

Rib 3 more rows.

Cast off in rib.

## COLLAR

Join shoulder seams.

With right side facing and 3.25mm needles, slip 7(8:8:9:9) sts from right front holder onto a needle, pick up and k13 sts up right front neck, 26(28:28:30:30) sts across back neck and 13 sts down left front neck, then k7(8:8:9:9) sts from left front holder. 66(70:70:74:74) sts.

**Next row** K2, * p2, k2; rep from * to end.

**Next row** K4, * p2, k2; rep from * to last 6 sts, p2, k4.

These 2 rows set the rib with garter st borders.

**Next 2 rows** Patt to last 22 sts, turn.

**Next 2 rows** Patt to last 14 sts, turn.

**Next 2 rows** Patt to last 6 sts, turn.

**Next 2 rows** Patt to last 2 sts, turn.

**Next row** (wrong side) Patt to end.

Cast off in patt.

## TO MAKE UP

Sew sleeves into armholes, with row ends above coloured threads sewn to sts cast off at underarm. Join side and sleeve seams. Sew in zip. Sew on pocket. Sew on button for pocket.

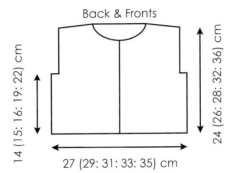

Back & Fronts

14 (15: 16: 19: 22) cm

27 (29: 31: 33: 35) cm

24 (26: 28: 32: 36) cm

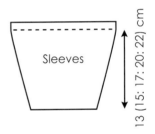

Sleeves

13 (15: 17: 20: 22) cm

# guernsey sweater

## MEASUREMENTS

To fit chest

92–97 97–102 102–107 107–112 112–114cm

Finished measurements

Chest

| 108 | 117 | 125 | 133 | 141cm |

Length

| 68 | 70 | 70 | 72 | 74cm |

Sleeve seam

| 54 | 54 | 55 | 55 | 56cm |

## MATERIALS

20(22:23:24:25) 50g balls Debbie Bliss
cotton dk in Teal

Pair of each size 3.75mm and 4mm knitting
needles

## TENSION

20 sts and 28 rows to 10cm square over st st
using 4mm needles.

## ABBREVIATIONS

alt = alternate; beg = beginning; cm =
centimetre; cont = continue; dec = decrease;
foll = following; inc = increase; k = knit;
m1 = make one st by picking up and working
into back of loop lying between st just worked
and next st; p = purl; patt = pattern;
rem = remaining; rep = repeat; st(s) = stitch(es);
st st = stocking stitch.

## BACK

** With 3.75mm needles, cast on
110(118:126:134:142) sts.

K 1 row.

**Next row** (right side) K2, [p2, k2] to end.

**Next row** P2, [k2, p2] to end.

Rep the last 2 rows until work measures
8cm from cast on edge, ending with a wrong
side row.

**Next row** (right side) Purl.

Change to 4mm needles.

**Next row** Knit.

Beg with a k row, work in st st until back
measures 44(45:45:45.5:47.5)cm from cast on
edge, ending with a p row.

### Shape armholes

Cast off 6 sts at beg of next 2 rows.

98(106:114:122:130) sts.

**Next row** (right side) Purl.

**Next row** Knit.

**Next row** (right side) K0(1:0:0:0), p0(2:1:2:1),
k0(1:1:2:1), p0(0:1:1:0), k0(0:2:1:0),
p0(0:2:1:0), k0(0:1:2:0), p0(0:0:2:0),
k0(0:0:1:0), * k2, p2, k2, p1, k1, p1, k2, p2,
k1; rep from * to last 0(4:8:12:2) sts,
k0(2:2:2:2), p0(2:2:2:0), k0(0:2:2:0),
p0(0:1:1:0), k0(0:1:1:0), p0(0:0:1:0),
k0(0:0:2:0), p0(0:0:1:0).

**Next row** P0(1:1:2:0), k0(2:2:2:1), p0(1:2:1:1),
k0(0:2:2:0), p0(0:1:2:0), k0(0:0:2:0),
p0(0:0:1:0), * k2, p2, k2, p1, k2, p2, k2, p1;
rep from * to last 0(4:8:12:2) sts, k0(2:2:2:2),
p0(2:2:2:0), k0(0:2:2:0), p0(0:1:1:0),
k0(0:1:2:0), p0(0:0:2:0), k0(0:0:1:0).

**Next row** P0(1:0:0:0), k0(2:3:2:1), p0(1:2:2:1),
k0(0:2:3:0), p0(0:1:2:0), k0(0:0:2:0),
p0(0:0:1:0), * k1, p1, k2, p2, k3, p2, k2, p1;
rep from * to last 0(4:8:12:2) sts, k0(1:1:1:1),
p0(1:1:1:1), k0(2:2:2:0), p0(0:2:2:0),
k0(0:2:3:0), p0(0:0:2:0), k0(0:0:1:0).

**Next row** K0(1:0:2:0), p0(3:3:5:2), k0(0:2:2:0),
p0(0:3:3:0),* p2, k2, p5, k2, p3; rep from * to
last 0(4:8:12:2) sts, p0(2:2:2:2), k0(2:2:2:0),
p0(0:4:5:0), k0(0:0:2:0), p0(0:0:1:0).

The last 4 rows form the yoke patt and are
repeated. **

Cont in patt until back measures
68(70:70:72:74)cm from cast on edge, ending
with a right side row.

**Next row** (wrong side) Cast off 31(35:38:42:45)
sts knitwise, k next 35(35:37:37:39) sts, then
cast off rem sts knitwise.

Leave centre 36(36:38:38:40) sts on a holder
for back neck.

## FRONT

Work as Back from ** to **.

Cont in patt until front measures
60(62:62:64:66)cm from cast on edge, ending
with a wrong side row.

### Shape neck

**Next row** (right side) Patt 41(45:48:51:54) sts,
turn and cont on these sts only, leave rem sts on
a spare needle.

Dec one st at neck edge of next 4 rows, and
then at same edge on every foll alt row until
31(35:38:42:45) sts rem. Cont straight for a few
rows until front measures same as Back to

shoulder, ending with a right side row.

Cast off knitwise.

With right side facing, slip 16(16:18:20:22) sts at centre front onto a holder, rejoin yarn to rem sts and patt to end.

Complete to match first side reversing shaping and ending with a right side row.

Cast off knitwise.

SLEEVES

With 3.75mm needles, cast on 50(50:54:54:54) sts.

K 1 row.

**1st row** (right side) K2, [p2, k2] to end.

**2nd row** P2, [k2, p2] to end.

Rep these 2 rows for 8cm, ending with a wrong side row and inc 4(4:4:6:8) sts evenly across last row. 54(54:58:60:62) sts.

**Next row** (right side) Purl.

Change to 4mm needles.

**Next row** (wrong side) Knit.

Beg with a k row, work 4 rows in st st.

**Next row** K2, m1, k to last 2 sts, m1, k2.

Work 5 rows.

**Next row** K2, m1, k to last 2 sts, m1, k2.

Work 3 rows.

Rep the last 10 rows until there are 98(102:102:108:110) sts.

Cont straight until sleeve measures 54(54:55:55:56)cm from beg, ending with a p row.

Mark each end of last row with coloured thread.

Beg with a k row work 9 rows in st st.

**Next row** (wrong side) Cast off knitwise.

COLLAR

Join right shoulder seam.

With right side facing and 3.75mm needles, pick up and k28(28:28:29:29) sts down left front

neck, k across 16(16:18:20:22) sts from front holder and inc 1 st in centre, pick up and k28(28:28:29:29) sts up right front neck, then k across 36(36:38:38:40) sts from back holder and inc 1 st in centre. 110(110:114:118:122) sts.

**Next row** (wrong side) Knit.

**Next row** Purl.

**1st rib row** (wrong side) P2, [k2, p2] to end.

**2nd rib row** K2, [p2, k2] to end.

Work in rib for a further 20cm, ending with a wrong side row.

**Next row** Knit.

Cast off purlwise.

TO MAKE UP

Join left shoulder and collar seam, reversing seam on last 12cm. Sew sleeves into armholes, with row ends above markers sewn to cast off sts at underarm. Join side and sleeve seams.

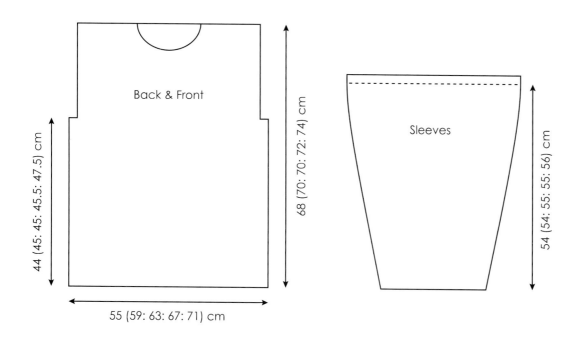

Back & Front

68 (70: 70: 72: 74) cm

44 (45: 45: 45.5: 47.5) cm

55 (59: 63: 67: 71) cm

Sleeves

54 (54: 55: 55: 56) cm

# striped cardigan

## MEASUREMENTS

To fit ages

| 3–4 | 5–6 | 7–8 | 9–10 years |
|---|---|---|---|

Finished measurements

Chest

| 70 | 75 | 85 | 90cm |
|---|---|---|---|

Length to shoulder

| 30 | 35 | 40 | 43cm |
|---|---|---|---|

Sleeve length

| 17 | 21 | 25 | 29cm |
|---|---|---|---|

## MATERIALS

3(3:4:5) 50g balls of Debbie Bliss cotton dk in
White (A), 3(3:4:4) 50g balls in Lime (B) and
2(2:2:3) 50g balls in Duck Egg (C)
Pair of each size 3.75mm and 4mm knitting
needles
6 buttons

## TENSION

20 sts and 28 rows to 10cm square over st st
using 4mm needles.

## ABBREVIATIONS

beg = beginning; cont = continue;
cm = centimetre; dec = decrease;
foll = following; inc = increase; k = knit;
p = purl; patt = pattern; rem = remaining;
rep = repeat; sl = slip; st(s) = stitch(es);
st st = stocking stitch; tog = together; yrn = yarn
round needle to make one st.

## BACK

With 3.75mm needles and C, cast on
72(77:87:92) sts.

**1st row** (right side) P2, * k3, p2; rep from
* to end.

**2nd row** P to end.

Rep the last 2 rows 4 times more.

Change to 4mm needles.

Beg with a k row work in st st and stripes of
4 rows A and 4 rows B until back measures
16(20:24:26)cm from cast on edge, ending with
a p row.

### Shape armholes

Cast off 6(7:8:9) sts at beg of next 2 rows.
60(63:71:74) sts.

Cont in st st until back measures
28(33:38:41)cm from cast on edge, ending with
a p row.

### Shape shoulders and back neck

**Next row** (right side) K20(21:23:24), turn,
and cont on these sts, leave rem sts on a
spare needle.

Dec one st at neck edge on the next 3 rows.
17(18:20:21) sts.

Work 4 rows straight.

Cast off.

With right side facing, slip centre 20(21:25:26)
sts onto a holder, rejoin yarn to rem sts, k
to end.

Dec one st at neck edge on the next 3 rows.
17(18:20:21) sts.

Work 4 rows straight.

Cast off.

## POCKET LININGS (make 2)

With 3.75mm needles and A, cast on
22(22:27:27) sts.

Beg with a k row work 21(21:25:25) rows st st.
Leave sts on a holder.

## LEFT FRONT

With 3.75mm needles and C, cast on
31(36:41:46) sts.

**1st row** (right side) P2, * k3, p2; rep from
* to last 4 sts, k4.

**2nd row** P to end.

Rep the last 2 rows 4 times more.

Change to 4mm needles.

Beg with a k row work in st st and stripes of
4 rows A and 4 rows B.

Work 20(20:24:24) rows.

### Place pocket

**Next row** (right side) K5(7:7:10) sts, place next
22(22:27:27) sts on a holder, k4(7:7:9).

**Next row** P4(7:7:9) sts, p across sts of one
pocket lining, p5(7:7:10).

Cont straight until front measures
16(20:24:26)cm from cast on edge, ending with
a p row.

### Shape armhole

Cast off 6(7:8:9) sts at beg of next row.
25(29:33:37) sts.

Cont in st st until front measures
21(25:29:32)cm from cast on edge, ending with
a p row.

### Shape neck

**Next row** (right side) K to last 3(4:5:6) sts, turn
and leave these sts on a holder.

Dec one st at neck edge on next 5(7:8:10) rows.
17(18:20:21) sts rem.

Work straight until front matches Back to shoulder, ending at side edge.

**Shape shoulder**

Cast off.

RIGHT FRONT

With 3.75mm needles and C, cast on 31(36:41:46) sts.

**1st row** (right side) K4, p2, * k3, p2; rep from * to end.

**2nd row** P to end.

Rep the last 2 rows 4 times more.

Change to 4mm needles.

Beg with a k row work in st st and stripes of 4 rows A and 4 rows B.

Work 20(20:24:24) rows.

**Place pocket**

**Next row** (right side) K4(7:7:9) sts, place next 22(22:27:27) sts on a holder, k5(7:7:10).

**Next row** P5(7:7:10) sts, p across sts of rem pocket lining, p4(7:7:9).

Cont straight until front measures 16(20:24:26)cm from cast on edge, ending with a k row.

**Shape armhole**

Cast off 6(7:8:9) sts at beg of next row. 25(29:33:37) sts.

Cont in st st until front measures 21(25:29:32)cm from cast on edge, ending with a p row.

Break off yarn.

**Shape neck**

**Next row** (right side) Slip first 3(4:5:6) sts onto a holder, rejoin yarn, k to end.

Dec one st at neck edge on next 5(7:8:10) rows.

17(18:20:21) sts rem.

Work straight until front matches Back to shoulder, ending at side edge.

**Shape shoulder**

Cast off.

SLEEVES

With 3.75mm needles and C, cast on 42(47:52:57) sts.

**1st row** (right side) P2, * k3, p2; rep from * to end.

**2nd row** P to end.

Rep the last 2 rows 4 times more.

Change to 4mm needles.

Beg with a k row, work in st st and stripes of 4 rows A and 4 rows B **at the same time** inc and work into st st one st at each end of 6th(4th:6th:6th) row and every foll 4th (6th:8th:10th) row until there are 56(59:64:69) sts.

Cont straight until sleeve measures 17(21:25:29)cm from cast on edge, ending with a p row.

Place markers at each end of last row.

Work a further 8(9:11:12) rows.

Cast off.

NECKBAND

Join shoulder seams.

With right side facing, 4mm needles and C, k3(4:5:6) sts from right front holder, pick up and k17(18:20:21) sts up right front neck, 8 sts from right back neck, k20(21:25:26) sts from back neck holder, pick up and k7 sts up left back neck, 17(18:20:21) sts down left front neck, then k3(4:5:6) sts from left front holder. 75(80:90:95) sts.

**1st row** (wrong side) P4, * k2, p3; rep from * to last 6 sts, k2, p4.

**2nd row** K to end.

Rep the last 2 rows once.

Change to 3.75mm needles.

Work 3 more rows.

Cast off, working k2tog over each garter st panel.

POCKET TOPS

With right side facing, 3.75mm needles and C, slip 22(22:27:27) sts from pocket front onto a needle.

**1st row** (right side) K to end.

**2nd row** P3, * k2, p3; rep from * to last 4 sts, k2, p2.

Rep the last 2 rows once more.

Cast off.

BUTTON BAND

With right side facing, 3.75mm needles and C, pick up and k55(60:70:75) sts evenly along left front edge.

**1st row** (wrong side) P4, * k2, p3; rep from * to last 6 sts, k2, p4.

**2nd row** K to end.

Rep the last 2 rows 3 times more and the 1st row again.

Cast off.

BUTTONHOLE BAND

With right side facing, 3.75mm needles and C, pick up and k55(60:70:75) sts evenly along right front edge.

**1st row** (wrong side) P4, * k2, p3; rep from * to last 6 sts, k2, p4.

**2nd row** K to end.

Rep the last 2 rows once more.

**Buttonhole row** Rib 2, [yrn, rib 2 tog, rib 8(9:11:12)] 5 times, yrn, rib 2 tog, rib 1.
Work 4 more rows.
Cast off.

TO MAKE UP
Sew sleeves into armholes, with row ends above markers sewn to sts cast off at underarm. Join side and sleeve seams. Sew down pocket linings and pocket tops.

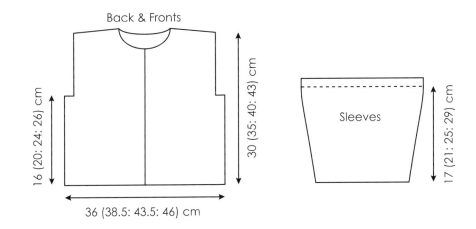

Back & Fronts

30 (35: 40: 43) cm

16 (20: 24: 26) cm

36 (38.5: 43.5: 46) cm

Sleeves

17 (21: 25: 29) cm

# jacket with patterned yoke

## MEASUREMENTS

To fit bust

| 87 | 92 | 97 | 102 | 107 | 112cm |

Finished measurements

Bust

| 94 | 98 | 102 | 110 | 114 | 18cm |

Length to shoulder

| 53 | 54 | 55 | 56 | 57 | 58cm |

Sleeve length

| 45 | 45 | 46 | 46 | 47 | 47cm |

## MATERIALS

13(14:15:16:17:18) 50g balls Debbie Bliss
cotton dk in White

Pair of each size 3.75mm and 4mm knitting
needles

45(45:45:45:45:50)cm open-ended zip

## TENSION

20 sts and 28 rows to 10cm square over st st
using 4mm needles.

## ABBREVIATIONS

alt = alternate; beg = beginning; cm =
centimetre; cont = continue; dec = decrease;
foll = following; inc = increase;
k = knit; m1 = make one st by picking up and
working into back of loop lying between st just
worked and next st; p = purl; patt = pattern;
rem = remaining; rep = repeat; skpo = sl 1, k1,
pass slipped st over; sl = slip; st(s) = stitch(es);
st st = stocking stitch; tog = together.

## BACK

With 3.75mm needles, cast on
94(98:102:110:114:118) sts.

**1st, 3rd, 4th and 6th sizes only**

**1st rib row** (right side) P2, * k2, p2; rep from
* to end.

**2nd rib row** K2, * p2, k2; rep from * to end.

**2nd and 5th sizes only**

**1st rib row** (right side) K2, * p2, k2; rep from
* to end.

**2nd rib row** P2, * k2, p2; rep from * to end.

**All sizes**

These 2 rows form the rib.

Rep the last 2 rows 12(12:13:13:14:14) times
more and inc 1 st at each end of last row.
96(100:104:112:116:120) sts.

Change to 4mm needles.

Beg with a k row work in st st.

Work 4 rows.

**Dec row** (right side) K3, skpo, k6, skpo, k to last
to last 13 sts, k2tog, k6, k2tog, k3.

Work 3 rows.

Rep the last 4 rows once more and the dec row
again. 84(88:92:100:104:108) sts.

Cont straight until back measures
19(19:20:20:21:21)cm from cast on edge,
ending with a p row.

**Inc row** (right side) K3, m1, k to last 3 sts,
m1, k3.

Work 5 rows.

Rep the last 6 rows four times more and the inc
row again. 96(100:104:112:116:120) sts.

Cont straight until back measures
32(32:33:33:34:34)cm from cast on edge,
ending with a p row.

**Next row** K4(1:3:2:4:1), p1, k1, p1, * k2, p1,
k1, p1; rep from * to last 4(1:3:2:4:1) sts,
k4(1:3:2:4:1).

**Next row** P5(2:4:3:5:2), * k1, p4; rep from * to
last 6(3:5:4:6:3) sts, k1, p5(2:4:3:5:2).

These 2 rows form the yoke patt and are
repeated.

Work 4 more rows.

## Shape armholes

Cast off 8(8:9:9:10:10) sts at beg of next
2 rows. 80(84:86:94:96:100) sts.

Dec one st at each end of the next row and
7(9:5:9:5:7) foll alt rows.
64(64:74:74:84:84) sts.

Cont straight until back measures
53(54:55:56:57:58)cm from cast on edge,
ending with a wrong side row.

## Shape shoulders

Cast off 11(11:12:12:13:13) sts at beg of next
2 rows and 11(11:13:13:14:14) sts at beg of foll
2 rows.

Cast off rem 20(20:24:24:30:30) sts.

## LEFT FRONT

With 3.75mm needles, cast on
47(49:51:55:57:59) sts.

**1st, 3rd, 4th and 6th sizes only**

**1st rib row** (right side) P2, * k2, p2; rep from
* to last 5 sts, k2, p1, k1, p1.

**2nd rib row** P1, k1, p3, k2, * p2, k2; rep from
* to end.

**2nd and 5th sizes only**

**1st rib row** (right side) * K2, p2; rep from

* to last 5 sts, k2, p1, k1, p1.

**2nd rib row** P1, k1, p3, * k2, p2; rep from
* to end.

**All sizes**

These 2 rows form the rib with moss st front
border and are repeated 12(12:13:13:14:14)
times more.

Change to 4mm needles.

**1st row** (right side) K to last 3 sts, p1, k1, p1.

**2nd row** P1, k1, p to end.

These 2 rows form the st st with moss st border.

Work a further 2 rows.

**Dec row** (right side) K3, skpo, k6, skpo, patt
to end.

Work 3 rows.

Rep the last 4 rows once more and the dec row
again. 41(43:45:49:51:53) sts.

Cont straight until front measures
19(19:20:20:21:21)cm from cast on edge,
ending with a wrong side row.

**Inc row** (right side) K3, m1, patt to end.

Work 5 rows.

Rep the last 6 rows four times more and the inc
row again. 47(49:51:55:57:59) sts.

Cont straight until front measures
32(32:33:33:34:34)cm from cast on edge,
ending with a wrong side row.

**Next row** (right side) K4(1:3:2:4:1), p1, k1, p1,
* k2, p1, k1, p1; rep from * to end.

**Next row** P1, * k1, p4; rep from * to last
6(3:5:4:6:3) sts, k1, p5(2:4:3:5:2).

These 2 rows form the yoke patt and are
repeated.

Work 4 more rows.

**Shape armhole**

Cast off 8(8:9:9:10:10) sts at beg of next row.
39(41:42:46:47:49) sts

Work 1 row.

Dec one st at beg of the next row and
7(9:5:9:5:7) foll alt rows.

31(31:36:36:41:41) sts.

Cont straight until front measures
47(48:48:49:49:50)cm from cast on edge,
ending with a wrong side row.

**Shape neck**

**Next row** (right side) Patt to last
8(9:10:11:12:13) sts, turn and leave these sts
on a holder.

Dec one st at neck edge on next 1(0:1:0:2:1)
rows. 22(22:25:25:27:27) sts rem.

Work straight until front matches Back to
shoulder, ending at armhole edge.

**Shape shoulder**

Cast off 11(11:12:12:13:13) sts at beg of next row.

Work 1 row.

Cast off rem 11(11:13:13:14:14) sts.


RIGHT FRONT

With 3.75mm needles, cast on
47(49:51:55:57:59) sts.

**1st, 3rd, 4th and 6th sizes only**

**1st rib row** (right side) P1, k1, p1 * k2, p2; rep
from * to end.

**2nd rib row** * K2, * p2, k2; rep from * to last
5 sts, p3, k1, p1.

**2nd and 5th sizes only**

**1st rib row** (right side) P1, k1, p1, * k2, p2;
rep from * to last 2 sts, k2.

**2nd rib row** P2, * k2, p2; rep from * to last
7 sts, k2, p3, k1, p1.

**All sizes**

These 2 rows form the rib with moss st front
border and are repeated 12(12:13:13:14:14)
times more.

Change to 4mm needles.

**1st row** (right side) P1, k1, p1, k to end.

**2nd row** P to last 2 sts, k1, p1.

These 2 rows form the st st with moss st border.
Work a further 2 rows.

**Dec row** (right side) Patt to last 13 sts, k2tog,
k6, k2tog, k3.

Work 3 rows.

Rep the last 4 rows once more and the dec row
again. 41(43:45:49:51:53) sts.

Cont straight until front measures
19(19:20:20:21:21)cm from cast on edge,
ending with a wrong side row.

**Inc row** (right side) Patt to last 3 sts, m1, k3.

Work 5 rows.

Rep the last 6 rows four times more and the inc
row again. 47(49:51:55:57:59) sts.

Cont straight until front measures
32(32:33:33:34:34)cm from cast on edge,
ending with a wrong side row.

**Next row** (right side) P1, k1, p1, * k2, p1, k1,
p1; rep from * to last 4(1:3:2:4:1) sts,
k4(1:3:2:4:1).

**Next row** P5(2:4:3:5:2), * k1, p4; rep from * to
last 2 sts, k1, p1.

These 2 rows form the yoke patt and are
repeated.

Work 5 more rows.

**Shape armhole**

Cast off 8(8:9:9:10:10) sts at beg of next row.
39(41:42:46:47:49) sts.

Dec one st at end of the next row and
7(9:5:9:5:7) foll alt rows.
31(31:36:36:41:41) sts.

Cont straight until front measures
47(48:48:49:49:50)cm from cast on edge,
ending with a wrong side row.

## Shape neck

**Next row** (right side) Patt 8(9:10:11:12:13) sts, leave these sts on a holder, patt to end.

Dec one st at neck edge on next 1(0:1:0:2:1) rows. 22(22:25:25:27:27) sts rem.

Work straight until front matches Back to shoulder, ending at armhole edge.

## Shape shoulder

Cast off 11(11:12:12:13:13) sts at beg of next row.

Work 1 row.

Cast off rem 11(11:13:13:14:14) sts.

## SLEEVES

With 3.75mm needles, cast on 42(46:50:54:58:62) sts.

**1st rib row** (right side) K2, *p2, k2; rep from * to end.

**2nd rib row** P2, * k2, p2; rep from * to end.

These 2 rows form the rib and are repeated 12(12:13:13:14:14) times more.

Change to 4mm needles.

Beg with a k row, work in st st.

Work 2 rows.

**Inc row** (right side) K3, m1, k to last 3 sts, m1, k3.

Work 7 rows.

Rep the last 8 rows 10 times more and the inc row again. 66(70:74:78:82:86) sts.

Cont straight until sleeve measures 45(145:46:46:47:47)cm from cast on edge, ending with a wrong side row.

## Shape sleeve top

Cast off 8(8:9:9:10:10) sts at beg of next 2 rows. 50(54:56:60:62:66) sts.

Dec 1 st at each end of the next 4(6:6:8:8:10) rows then 4 foll alt rows then every foll 4th row until 30 sts rem.

Cast off 2 sts at beg of next 10 rows.

Cast off rem 10 sts.

## COLLAR

Join shoulder seams.

With right side facing and 3.75mm needles, slip 8(9:10:11:12:13) sts from right front neck holder onto a needle, pick up and k20(20:21:21:22:22) sts up right front neck, cast on 32(35:36:39:40:43) sts pick up and k20(20:21:21:22:22) sts down left front neck, then patt 8(9:10:11:12:13) sts from left front holder. 88(93:98:103:108:113) sts.

**1st patt row** (right side) P1, k1, p1, * k2, p1, k1, p1; rep from * to end.

**2nd patt row** P1, k1, * p4, k1; rep from * to last st, p1.

**Next 2 rows** Patt to last 30 sts, turn.

**Next 2 rows** Patt to last 25 sts, turn.

**Next 2 rows** Patt to last 20 sts, turn.

**Next 2 rows** Patt to last 15 sts, turn.

**Next 2 rows** Patt to last 10 sts, turn.

**Next 2 rows** Patt to last 5 sts, turn.

**Next row** Patt to end.

Change to 4mm needles.

Cont in patt across all sts for a further 8cm.

Cast off in patt.

## TO MAKE UP

Join side and sleeve seams. Sew cast on edge of collar to cast off edge of back neck, easing to fit. Sew sleeves into armholes. Sew in zip.

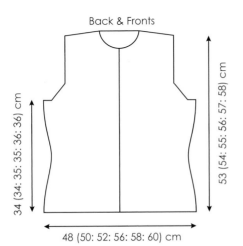

Back & Fronts

34 (34: 35: 35: 36: 36) cm

53 (54: 55: 56: 57: 58) cm

48 (50: 52: 56: 58: 60) cm

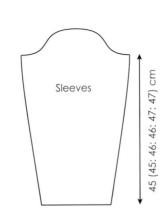

Sleeves

45 (45: 46: 46: 47: 47) cm

# striped hat

### SIZE

To fit age 3–12 months.

### MATERIALS

One 50g ball of Debbie Bliss cotton dk in each
of Teal (A) and White (B)
Set of four 4mm double-pointed knitting needles

### TENSION

20 sts and 28 rows to 10cm square over st st
using 4mm needles.

### ABBREVIATIONS

cm = centimetre; dec = decrease; rep = repeat;
st(s) = stitch(es); st st = stocking stitch;
tog = together.

### TO MAKE

With 4mm needles and A, cast on 70 sts and
divide these sts onto 3 needles.
Mark end of cast on row to denote end of
rounds.
K8 rounds, so forming st st.
Cont in st st working stripes of 4 rounds in B,
4 rounds in A throughout.
Work 21 rounds.
**Dec round** [K2tog, k8] 7 times. 63 sts.
K 3 rounds.
**Dec round** [K2tog, k7] 7 times. 56 sts.
K 3 rounds.
**Dec round** [K2tog, k6] 7 times. 49 sts.
K 3 rounds.
**Dec round** [K2tog, k5] 7 times. 42 sts.
K 3 rounds.
**Dec round** [K2tog] 21 times. 21 sts.
Break yarn and thread through sts, do not
pull up.

### STALK

With two double-pointed 4mm needles, cast on
5 sts.
K 1 row.
Slide these 5 sts to the opposite end of the same
needle, place needle in left hand and bringing
yarn firmly from last st to first st, k5 sts.
Rep the last row for 3cm.
Break yarn, thread through sts, pull up
and secure.
Insert cast on edge of stalk into top of hat, pull
up hat sts around stalk and stitch in place.

# patchwork aran jacket

## MEASUREMENTS

To fit bust

81–97     102–117cm

Finished measurements

Bust

107     127cm

Length

51     53cm

Sleeve length

45     48cm

## MATERIALS

20(23) 50g balls of Debbie Bliss cotton dk in
Pale Duck Egg

Pair of each size 4mm and 4.5mm knitting
needles

Cable needle

Optional decorative pin to fasten

## TENSION

20 sts and 29 rows to 10cm square over moss
st using 4.5mm needles.

## ABBREVIATIONS

alt = alternate; beg = beginning; C4B = slip next
2 sts onto cable needle and hold at back of
work, k2, then k2 from cable needle; C6B = slip
next 3 sts onto cable needle and hold at back of
work, k3, then k3 from cable needle; C6F = slip
next 3 sts onto cable needle and hold to front of
work, k3, then k3 from cable needle;
Cr3B = slip next 2 sts onto cable needle and
hold at back of work, k1, then slip centre st from
cable needle back onto left hand needle and
purl it, then k1 from cable needle; Cr3F = slip
next 2 sts onto cable needle and hold to front of
work, k1, then slip centre st from cable needle
back onto left hand needle and purl it, then k1
from cable needle; C5R = slip next 2 sts onto
cable needle and hold at back of work, k3, then
p2 from cable needle; C5L = slip next 3 sts onto
cable needle and hold to front of work, p2, then
k3 from cable needle; cm = centimetre;
cont = continue; dec = decrease;
foll = following; inc = increase; k = knit;
kfb = k into front and back of next st;
m1 = make one st by picking up and working
into back of loop lying between st just worked
and next st; m1p = make one st purlwise;
p = purl; patt = pattern; pfb = p into front and
back of next st; rem = remaining; rep = repeat;
st(s) = stitch(es); tog = together.

## PATT PANEL A (worked over 15 sts)

**1st row** (right side) K1, [p1, k1] 7 times.

**2nd, 4th and 6th rows** P1, [k1, p1] 7 times.

**3rd row** Cr3B, [p1, Cr3B] 3 times.

**5th row** As 1st row.

**7th row** K1, [p1, Cr3F] 3 times, p1, k1.

**8th row** As 2nd row.

These 8 rows form Patt Panel A and are
repeated.

## PATT PANEL B (worked over 20 sts)

**1st row** (right side) K3, p4, k6, p4, k3.

**2nd and all wrong side rows** K all k sts and p
all p sts as they appear.

**3rd row** K3, p4, C6F, p4, k3.

**5th row** As 1st row.

**7th row** C5L, p2, k6, p2, C5R.

**9th row** P2, C5L, C6F, C5R, p2.

**11th row** P4, C6B, C6B, p4.

**13th row** P2, C5R, C6F, C5L, p2.

**15th row** C5R, p2, k6, p2, C5L.

**16th row** As 2nd row.

These 16 rows form Patt Panel B and are
repeated.

## PATT PANEL C (worked over 13 sts)

**1st row** (right side) K2, p2, k2, p1, k2, p2, k2.

**2nd row** P1, k2, p2, k3, p2, k2, p1.

**3rd row** P2, k2, p2, k1, p2, k2, p2.

**4th row** K1, p2, k2, p3, k2, p2, k1.

These 4 rows form Patt Panel C and are
repeated.

PATT PANEL D (worked over 34 sts)

**1st row** (right side) P2, k6, [p6, k6] twice, p2.

**2nd and all wrong side rows** K all k sts and p all p sts as they appear.

**3rd row** P2, k6, p6, C6F, p6, k6, p2.

**5th row** As 1st row.

**7th row** P2, C6F, p6, k6, p6, C6F, p2.

**9th row** As 3rd row.

**11th row** C5R, C5L, [p2, C5R, C5L] twice.

**13th row** K3, p4, k3, C5R, p4, C5L, k3, p4, k3.

**15th row** K3, p4, C6B, p8, C6B, p4, k3.

**17th row** K3, p4, k3, C5L, p4, C5R, k3, p4, k3.

**19th row** C5L, C5R, [p2, C5L, C5R] twice.

**21st row** As 3rd row.

**23rd row** As 7th row.

**24th row** As 2nd row.

These 24 rows form Patt Panel D and are repeated.

BACK

With 4.5mm needles, cast on 116(136) sts.

**1st row** (right side) P1, [k1, p1] 2(7) times, [p2, k2] 26 times, p3, [k1, p1] 2(7) times.

**2nd row** P1, [k1, p1] 2(7) times, [k2, p2] 26 times, k2, [p1, k1] 2(7) times, p1.

Rep these 2 rows once more, then the 1st row again.

**Inc row** (wrong side) [P1, k1] 3(8) times, k1, p2, [k2, p2] 3 times, k2, pfb, m1p, p1, [k2, p1, m1p, p1] twice, kfb, m1, k1, [p1, m1p, p1, k2] twice, p2, k2, p2, k2tog, [p2, k2] twice, [pfb, m1p, p1, k2] twice, [p1, m1p, p1, k1, m1, k1] 5 times, p1, m1p, p1, [k2, p2] twice, k2tog, [p2, k2] twice, pfb, m1p, p1, k2, p1, [k1, p1] 2(7) times. 139(159) sts.

Now work in patt as follows:

**1st row** (right side) P1, [k1, p1] 2(7) times, p2,
k4, p2, work across 13 sts of 1st row of Patt Panel C, p1, work across 34 sts of 1st row of Patt Panel D, p2, [k4, p2] twice, work across 13 sts of 1st row of Patt Panel C, p2, work across 20 sts of 1st row of Patt Panel B, p2, k4, p2, work across 15 sts of 1st row of Patt Panel A, p2, [k1, p1] 2(7) times.

**2nd row** [P1, k1] 3(8) times, work 2nd row Patt Panel A, k2, p4, k2, work 2nd row Patt Panel B, k2, work 2nd row Patt Panel C, k2, [p4, k2] twice, work 2nd row of Patt Panel D, k1, work 2nd row Patt Panel C, k2, p4, k1, [k1, p1] 3(8) times.

**3rd row** P1, [k1, p1] 2(7) times, p2, C4B, p2, work 3rd row Patt Panel C, p1, work 3rd row Patt Panel D, p2, [C4B, p2] twice, work 3rd row Patt Panel C, p2, work 3rd row Patt Panel B, p2, C4B, p2, work 3rd row Patt Panel A, p2, [k1, p1] 2(7) times.

**4th row** As 2nd row but working 4th row of patt panels.

These 4 rows **set** the position of the Patt Panels and **form** the rope cables and the moss st side edges and are repeated, working the correct patt panel rows.

Cont in patt until 2 repeats and 3 rows of 3rd repeat (51 rows) of Patt Panel D have been worked, so ending with a right side row.

**Dec row** (wrong side) Patt 6(16), [p2tog, patt 2, p2tog, patt 3] twice, p2tog, patt 3, p2tog, patt 5, p2tog, patt 2, p2tog, patt 5, p2tog, patt 18, p2tog, patt 4, p2tog, patt 5, [p2tog, p2] 8 times, patt 17, p2tog, patt 8(18). 119(139) sts.

Change to 4mm needles.

K 5 rows.

**Inc row** (wrong side) K8(18), m1, k20, [m1, k5] twice, m1, k4, m1, k2, m1, k3, m1, k4, m1, k3,
m1, k2, [m1, k4] 3 times, [m1, k6, m1, k4] twice, k13, [m1, k3, m1, k5] twice, k2(12). 139(159) sts.

Change to 4.5mm needles and work in patt as follows:

**1st row** (right side) P1, [k1, p1] 2(7) times, p2, work across 15 sts of 1st row of Patt Panel A, p2, work across 13 sts of 1st row of Patt Panel C, p2, work across 20 sts of 1st row of Patt Panel B, p2, k4, p1, work across 34 sts of 1st row of Patt Panel D, p1, [k4, p2] twice, work across 13 sts of 1st row of Patt Panel C, p2, k4, p3, [k1, p1] 2(7) times.

**2nd row** [P1, k1] 3(8) times, k1, p4, k2, work 2nd row Patt Panel C, [k2, p4] twice, k1, work 2nd row Patt Panel D, k1, p4, k2, work 2nd row Patt Panel B, k2, work 2nd row of Patt Panel C, k2, work 2nd row Patt Panel A, k1, [k1, p1] 3(8) times.

**3rd row** P1, [k1, p1] 2(7) times, p2, work 3rd row Patt Panel A, p2, work 3rd row Patt Panel C, p2, work 3rd row Patt Panel B, p2, C4B, p1, work 3rd row Patt Panel D, p1, [C4B, p2] twice, work 3rd row Patt Panel C, p2, C4B, p3, [k1, p1] 2(7) times.

**4th row** As 2nd row but working 4th row of patt panels.

These 4 rows **re-set** the position of the patt panels and **re-form** the rope cables and the moss st side edges and are repeated, working the correct patt panel rows.

Cont straight in patt as now set until 5 repeats of Patt Panel B and the first 5(11) rows of the 6th repeat (85(91) rows) have been worked after last inc row, so ending with a right side row.

**Dec row** (wrong side) [P1, k1] 3(8) times, p2tog, k1, p1, k2tog, p1, k1, p1, k2tog, p1, k1, [p2tog, k1] twice, p1, k1, p2tog, k1, p1, k2tog, p2tog, k1, p2tog, patt 63, p1, k2tog, [p1, k1] twice, p2tog, [k1, p1] twice, [k2tog, p1] 7 times, [k1, p1] 2(7) times. 121(141) sts.

**Next row** P1, [k1, p1] 14(19) times, patt 63, [p1, k1] 14(19) times, p1.

Rep the last row 3 times more.

### Shape shoulders

Cast off 29(39) sts in moss st at beg of next 2 rows. 63 sts.

Cont straight in patt on rem sts for a further 5cm, ending with a wrong side row.

**Dec row** (right side) [P2tog, k1] twice, [p1, k2tog] 3 times, [p1, k1] 3 times, [p2tog, k1] 3 times, [p1, k2tog] 3 times, p1, [k1, p1] twice, k2tog, p1, [k1, p2tog] 3 times, k1, p1, k2tog, p1, k1, p1. 47 sts.

**Next row** P1, [k1, p1] to end.

Rep the last row 3 times more.

Cast off in moss st.

LEFT FRONT

With 4.5mm needles, cast on 67(77) sts.

**1st row** (right side) P1, [k1, p1] 2(7) times, [p2, k2] 14 times, p2, [k1, p1] twice.

**2nd row** [P1, k1] 3 times, [p2, k2] 14 times, [p1, k1] 2(7) times, p1.

Rep these 2 rows once more, then the 1st row again.

**Inc row** (wrong side) [P1, k1] 3 times, p2, k2, p2, k2tog, [p2, k2] twice, pfb, m1p, p1, k2, p1, m1p, p1, k1, m1, k1, p1, m1p, p1, k2, p1, m1p, p1, k1, m1, k1, p1, m1p, p1, k2, pfb, m1p, p1, [k2, p2] 4 times, k2, [p1, k1] 2(7) times, p1. 76(86) sts.

Now work in patt as follows:

**1st row** (right side) [P1, k1] 2(7) times, p2,

work across 15 sts of 1st row of Patt Panel A, p2, k4, p2, work across 20 sts of 1st row of Patt Panel B, p2, k4, p2, work across 13 sts of 1st row of Patt Panel C, p2, [k1, p1] twice.

**2nd row** [P1, k1] 3 times, work 2nd row Patt Panel C, k2, p4, k2, work 2nd row Patt Panel B, k2, p4, k2, work 2nd row Patt Panel A, [k1, p1] 3(8) times.

**3rd row** [P1, k1] 2(7) times, p2, work 3rd row Patt Panel A, p2, C4B, p2, work 3rd row Patt Panel B, p2, C4B, p2, work 3rd row Patt Panel C, p2, [k1, p1] twice.

**4th row** As 2nd row, but working 4th row of patt panels.

These 4 rows **set** the position of the Patt Panels and **form** the rope cables and the moss st side and front edges and are repeated, working the correct patt panel rows.

Cont in patt until 2 repeats and 3 rows of 3rd repeat (35 rows) of Patt Panel B have been worked, so ending with a right side row.

**Dec row** (wrong side) Patt 22, p2tog, patt 3,

[p2tog, p2tog, patt 4] twice, p2tog, p2tog, patt 3, p2tog, patt 24(34). 68(78) sts.

Change to 4mm needles.

K 5 rows.

**Inc row** (wrong side) K38, m1, [k2, m1] 3 times, k3, m1, k6, m1, k2, m1, k6, m1, k7(17). 76(86) sts.

Change to 4.5mm needles and work in patt as follows:

**1st row** (right side) [P1, k1] 2(7) times, p2, work across 20 sts of 1st row of Patt Panel B, p2, [k4, p2] twice, work across 15 sts of 1st row of Patt Panel A, p2, work across 13 sts of 1st row of Patt Panel C, p2, [k1, p1] twice.

**2nd row** [P1, k1] 3 times, work 2nd row Patt Panel C, k2, work 2nd row Patt Panel A, k2, [p4, k2] twice, work 2nd row Patt Panel B, [k1, p1] 3(8) times.

**3rd row** [P1, k1] 2(7) times, p2, work 3rd row of Patt Panel B, p2, [C4B, p2] twice, work 3rd row Patt Panel A, p2, work 3rd row Patt Panel C, p2, [k1, p1] twice.

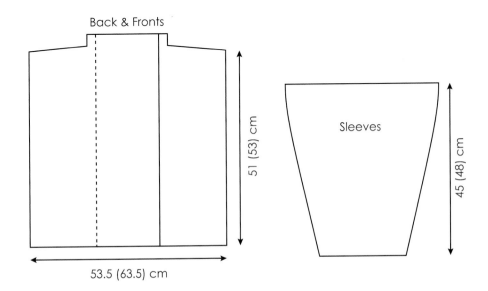

Back & Fronts

51 (53) cm

53.5 (63.5) cm

Sleeves

45 (48) cm

**4th row** As 2nd row, but working the 4th row of patt panels.

These 4 rows **re-set** the position of the patt panels and **re-form** the rope cables and the moss st side and front edges.

Cont straight in patt as now set until 6 repeats of Patt Panel B and the first 5(11) rows of the 7th repeat have been worked after last inc row, so ending with a right side row.

**Dec row** (wrong side) Patt 37, p1, k2tog, p1, k1, p2tog, k1, p1, [k2tog, p1] 3 times, k1, [p2tog, k1] 3 times, [p1, k2tog] twice, [p1, k1] 2(7) times, p1. 66(76) sts.

**Next row** P1, [k1, p1] 14(19) times, patt 37.

**Next row** Patt 37, [p1, k1] 14(19) times, p1.

Rep the last 2 rows once more.

### Shape shoulder

**Next row** Cast off 29(39) sts in moss st, patt to end.

Cont straight in patt on rem 37 sts for a further 5cm, ending with a wrong side row.

**Dec row** (right side) P1, [k2tog, p1] 6 times, [k1, p1] 9 times. 31 sts.

**Next row** P1, [k1, p1] to end.

Rep the last row 3 times more.

Cast off in moss st.


RIGHT FRONT

With 4.5mm needles, cast on 67(77) sts.

**1st row** (right side) P1, [k1, p1] twice, [p2, k2] 14 times, p2, [k1, p1] 2(7) times.

**2nd row** [P1, k1] 3(8) times, [p2, k2] 14 times, p1, [k1, p1] twice.

Rep these 2 rows once more, then the 1st row again.

**Inc row** (wrong side) [P1, k1] 3(8) times, [p1, m1p, p1, k2] twice, p1, m1p, p1, k1, m1, k1,

pfb, pfb, [k2, p2] twice, k2tog, [p2, k2] twice, [p1, m1p, p1, k1, m1, k1] twice, p1, m1p, p1, k2, [p1, m1p, p1, k1, m1, k1] twice, p2, k2, [p1, k1] twice, p1. 81(91) sts.

Now work in patt as follows:

**1st row** (right side) [P1, k1] twice, p2, work across 34 sts of 1st row of Patt Panel D, work across 13 sts of 1st row of Patt Panel C, p2, k4, p1, work across 15 sts of 1st row of Patt Panel A, p2, [k1, p1] 2(7) times.

**2nd row** [P1, k1] 3(8) times, work 2nd row Patt Panel A, k1, p4, k2, work 2nd row Patt Panel C, work 2nd row Patt Panel D, [k1, p1] 3 times.

**3rd row** (right side) [P1, k1] 2(7) times, p2, work 3rd row Patt Panel D, work 3rd row Patt Panel C, p2, C4B, p1, work 3rd row Patt Panel A, p2, [k1, p1] twice.

**4th row** As 2nd row, but working 4th row of patt panels.

These 4 rows **set** the position of the Patt Panels and **form** the rope cables and the moss st side and front edges and are repeated, working the correct patt panel rows.

Cont in patt until 2 repeats and 3 rows of 3rd repeat (51 rows) of Patt Panel D have been worked, so ending with a right side row.

**Dec row** (wrong side) Patt 6(16), p2tog, patt 2, p2tog, patt 3, [p2tog, patt 2] twice, p2tog, patt 18, [p2tog, patt 2] 8 times, patt 6. 68(78) sts.

Change to 4mm needles.

K 5 rows.

**Inc row** (wrong side) K8(18), m1, [k3, m1] twice, k4, m1, k2, m1, k4, m1, k3, m1, k18, m1, k23. 76(86) sts.

Change to 4.5mm needles and work in patt as follows:

**1st row** (right side) [P1, k1] twice, p2, work

across 13 sts of 1st row of Patt Panel C, p2, k4, p2, work across 15 sts of 1st row of Patt Panel A, p1, work across 20 sts of 1st row of Patt Panel B, p2, k4, p3, [k1, p1] 2(7) times.

**2nd row** [P1, k1] 3(8) times, k1, p4, k2, work 2nd row Patt Panel B, k1, work 2nd row Patt Panel A, k2, p4, k2, work 2nd row patt Panel C, [k1, p1] 3 times.

**3rd row** [P1, k1] twice, p2, work 3rd row Patt Panel C, p2, C4B, p2, work 3rd row Patt Panel A, p1, work 3rd row Patt Panel B, p2, C4B, p3, [k1, p1] 2(7) times.

**4th row** As 2nd row but working 4th row of patt panels.

These 4 rows **re-set** the position of the patt panels and **re-form** the rope cables and the moss st side and front edges.

Cont straight in patt as now set until 5 repeats of Patt Panel B and 5(11) rows of 6th repeat have been worked from last inc row, so ending with a wrong side row.

**Dec row** (right side) Patt 38, [p1, k2tog] twice, p1, k1, [p2tog, k1] 5 times, p1, k1, p1, k2tog, p1, k1, p2tog, [k1, p1] 3(8) times. 67(77) sts.

**Next row** P1, [k1, p1] 14(19) times, patt 38.

**Next row** Patt 38, [p1, k1] 14(19) times, p1.

Rep the last 2 rows once more.

### Shape shoulder

**Next row** (wrong side) Cast off 29(39) sts in moss st, patt to end.

Cont straight in patt on rem 38 sts for a further 5cm, ending with a right side row.

**Dec row** (wrong side) P1, [k2tog, p1] 7 times, [k1, p1] 8 times. 31 sts.

**Next row** P1, [k1, p1] to end.

Rep the last row 3 times more.

Cast off in moss st.

## SLEEVES

With 4.5mm needles, cast on 46 sts.

**1st row** (right side) [P1, k1] twice, [p2, k2] 9 times, p2, [k1, p1] twice.

**2nd row** [P1, k1] twice, [k2, p2] 9 times, k2, [k1, p1] twice.

Rep these 2 rows twice more and the 1st row again.

**Inc row** (wrong side) [P1, k1] twice, k2, pfb, m1p, p1, k2, [p1, m1p, p1, k2] twice, p2, k1, m1, k1, p2, k1, m1, k1, p2, [k2, p1, m1p, p1] twice, k2, pfb, m1p, p1, k2, [k1, p1] twice. 56 sts.

Now work in patt as follows:

**1st row** (right side) [P1, k1] twice, p2, k4, p1, work across 34 sts of 1st row of Patt Panel D, p1, k4, p2, [k1, p1] twice.

**2nd row** [P1, k1] 3 times, p4, k1, work 2nd row Patt Panel D, k1, p4, [k1, p1] 3 times.

**3rd row** (right side) [P1, k1] twice, p2, C4B, p1, work 3rd row Patt Panel D, p1, C4B, p2, [k1, p1] twice.

**4th row** As 2nd row, but working 4th row of patt panel.

These 4 rows **set** the position of the patt panel and **form** the rope cables and moss st to each side.

Cont in patt, working correct patt panel rows and inc 1 st at each end of 5th and every foll 5th row, until there are 92(100) sts, taking all inc sts into moss st.

Cont straight until sleeve measures 44(46)cm from cast on edge, ending with a right side row.

**Dec row** (wrong side) [P1, k1] 11(13) times, p1, p2tog, p2, p2tog, k2, p2tog, p2, p2tog, k3, k2tog, k1, p2, p2tog, p2, k1, k2tog, k3, p2tog, p2, p2tog, k2, p2tog, p2, p2tog, p1, [k1, p1] 11(13) times. 81(89) sts.

**Next row** P1, [k1, p1] to end.

Rep this row 4 times more.

Cast off in moss st.

## TO MAKE UP

Join shoulder seams. Matching centre of cast off edge of sleeve to shoulder, sew on sleeves. Join side and sleeve seams. Use pin to fasten.

# PICNIC

Simple ribs and easy, relaxed styles in perfect pastels and sharp, apple-green are lovely for the long, lazy days of summer, and make an evocative collection of designs for every member of the family.

# baby's ballerina top

## MEASUREMENTS

To fit ages

| 3–6 | 6–9 | 9–12 | 12–18 months |

Finished measurements

Chest

| 50 | 54 | 60 | 63cm |

Length

| 20 | 22 | 24 | 26cm |

Sleeve length

| 15 | 17 | 19 | 22cm |

## MATERIALS

3(3:4:5) 50g balls of Debbie Bliss baby
cashmerino in Mulberry

Pair of 3.25mm knitting needles

2m of 1-cm wide satin ribbon

## TENSION

25 sts and 34 rows to 10cm square over st st
using 3.25mm needles.

## ABBREVIATIONS

alt = alternate; beg = beginning;
cm = centimetre; cont = continue;
dec = decrease; foll = following; inc = increase;
k = knit; m1 = make one st by picking up and
working into back of loop lying between st just
worked and next st; p = purl; patt = pattern;
rem = remaining; rep = repeat; sl = slip;
st(s) = stitch(es); ssk = slip next 2 sts knitwise,
place tip of left hand needle into fronts of
slipped sts and k2tog; st st = stocking stitch; tbl
= through back loop; tog = together.

## BACK

With 3.25mm needles, cast on
145(154:172:181) sts.

**1st row** (right side) K.

**Dec row** P1, [p2tog, p1] to end.
97(103:115:121) sts.

K1 row.

**Dec row** P1, [p2tog, p1] to end. 65(69:77:81)
sts.

Beg with a k row, work in st st.

Cont until back measures 10(11:12:13)cm from
beg, ending with a p row.

**Shape armholes**

Cast off 4 sts at beg of next 2 rows.

57(61:69:73) sts.

Cont straight until back measures
20(22:24:26)cm, ending with a p row.

**Shape shoulders**

Cast off 13(14:17:18) sts at beg of next 2 rows.

31(33:35:37) sts.

Cast off purlwise.

## LEFT FRONT

With 3.25mm needles, cast on
143(152:161:170) sts.

**1st row** (right side) K.

**Dec row** K3, p1, [p2tog, p1] to last st, p1.
97(103:109:115) sts.

K 1 row.

**Dec row** K3, p1, [p2tog, p1] to end.
66(70:74:78) sts.

**Next row** K.

**Next row** K3, p to end.

Rep the last 2 rows until front measures 5cm,

ending with a k row.

**Shape front slope**

**Next row** (wrong side) Cast off 4 sts, p to end.
62(66:70:74) sts.

**Next row** K to last 3 sts, k2tog, k1.

**Next row** P1, p2tog, p to end.

Rep the last 2 rows until front measures
10(11:12:13)cm from cast on edge, ending with
a wrong side row.

**Shape armhole**

**Next row** Cast off 4 sts, k to last 3 sts,
k2tog, k1.

Keeping armhole edge straight, cont to dec 1 st
at front edge on every row as before until
13(14:17:18) sts rem.

Cont straight until front measures
20(22:24:26)cm, ending with a p row.

Cast off for shoulder.

RIGHT FRONT

With 3.25mm needles, cast on
143(152:161:170) sts.

**1st row** (right side) K.

**Dec row** P2, [p2tog, p1] to last 3 sts, k3.
97(103:109:115) sts.

K 1 row.

**Dec row** P1, [p2tog, p1] to last 3 sts, k3.
66(70:74:78) sts.

**Next row** K.

**Next row** P to last 3 sts, k3.

Rep the last 2 rows until front measures 5cm,
ending with a wrong side row.

**Shape front slope**

**Next row** (right side) Cast off 4 sts, k to end.
62(66:70:74) sts.

**Next row** P to last 3 sts, p2tog tbl, p1.

**Next row** K1, ssk, k to end.

Rep the last 2 rows until front measures
10(11:12:13)cm from cast on edge, ending with
a right side row.

**Shape armhole**

**Next row** (wrong side) Cast off 4 sts, p to last
3 sts, p2tog tbl, p1.

Keeping armhole edge straight, cont to dec at
front edge on every row as before until
13(14:17:18) sts rem.

Cont straight until front measures
20(22:24:26)cm, ending with a k row.

Cast off for shoulder.

SLEEVES

With 3.25mm needles, cast on 85(85:94:94) sts.

**1st row** (right side) K.

**Dec row** P2, [p2tog, p1] to last 2 sts, p2.
58(58:64:64) sts.

K 1 row.

**Dec row** P1, [p2tog, p1] to end. 39(39:43:43) sts.

Beg with a k row, work in st st.

Inc 1 st at each end of 3rd and every foll 6th
row until there are 51(55:61:65) sts.

Cont straight until sleeve measures
15(17:19:22)cm from cast on edge, ending with
a p row.

Mark each end of last row then work a further
6 rows.

Cast off.

TO MAKE UP

Join shoulder seams. Sew sleeves into armholes
with row ends above markers sewn to sts cast
off at underarm. Join side and sleeve seams,
leaving a 1cm gap in the right side seam 4.5cm
above cast on edge. Sew ribbon behind front
and back neck edges. Overlap left front with
right front, pass left front ribbon end through
gap in side seam and tie with right front ribbon.

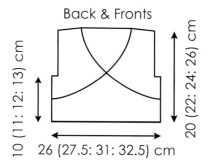

Back & Fronts

10 (11: 12: 13) cm

20 (22: 24: 26) cm

26 (27.5: 31: 32.5) cm

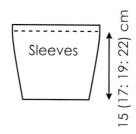

Sleeves

15 (17: 19: 22) cm

# jacket with ribbed yoke

## MEASUREMENTS

To fit ages

| 5–6 | 7–8 | 9–10 | 11–12 years |
|---|---|---|---|

Finished measurements

Chest

| 72 | 80 | 88 | 92cm |
|---|---|---|---|

Length to shoulder

| 54 | 58 | 63 | 69cm |
|---|---|---|---|

Sleeve length

| 31 | 35 | 39 | 43cm |
|---|---|---|---|

## MATERIALS

10(11:12:13) 50g balls of Debbie Bliss
cashmerino dk in Pale Blue
Pair of each size 3.75mm and 4mm knitting
needles
3(3:4:4) buttons

## TENSION

22 sts and 30 rows over st st and 28 sts and 30
rows to 10cm square over rib when slightly
stretched, both using 4mm needles.

## ABBREVIATIONS

beg = beginning; cont = continue; cm =
centimetres; dec = decrease; foll = following;
inc = increase; k = knit; p = purl; patt = pattern;
rem = remaining; rep = repeat; st(s) = stitch(es);
st st = stocking stitch; tog = together; yf = yarn
forward.

## BACK

With 3.75mm needles, cast on
102(114:126:138) sts.
K 3 rows.
Change to 4mm needles.
Beg with a k row work in st st.
Cont straight until back measures
34(36:39:42)cm from cast on edge, ending with
a p row.

**1st and 3rd sizes only**

**Next row** (right side) K2, * p2, k2; rep from
* to end.

**Next row** P2, * k2, p2; rep from * to end.

**2nd and 4th sizes only**

**Next row** (right side) P2, * k2, p2; rep from
* to end.

**Next row** K2, * p2, k2; rep from * to end.

These 2 rows form the rib patt and are repeated.

Cont straight until back measures
38(41:45:49)cm from cast on edge, ending with
a p row.

**Shape armholes**

Cast off 7(9:11:13) sts at beg of next 2 rows.
88(96:104:112) sts.
Continue straight until back measures
54(58:63:69)cm from cast on edge, ending with
a wrong side row.

**Shape shoulders**

Cast off 13(15:16:17) sts at beg of next 2 rows
and 14(15:16:18) sts at beg of foll 2 rows.
Cast off rem 34(36:40:42) sts tightly.

## LEFT FRONT

With 3.75mm needles, cast on 53(59:65:71) sts.
K 3 rows.
Change to 4mm needles.
**Next row** (right side) K to end.
**Next row** K3, p to end.
These 2 rows form the st st with garter st border.
Cont straight until front measures
34(36:39:42)cm from cast on edge, ending with
a wrong side row.

**1st and 3rd sizes only**

**Next row** (right side) K2, * p2, k2; rep from * to
last 7 sts, p2, k5.

**Next row** K3, p2, * k2, p2; rep from * to end.

**2nd and 4th sizes only**

**Next row** (right side) P2, * k2, p2; rep from * to
last 5 sts, k5.

**Next row** K3, * p2, k2; rep from * to end.

These 2 rows form the rib patt with garter
st border.
Cont straight until front measures
38(41:45:49)cm from cast on edge, ending with
a wrong side row.

**Shape armhole**

Cast off 7(9:11:13) sts at beg of next row.
46(50:54:58) sts.
Cont straight until front measures
49(53:57:63)cm from cast on edge, ending with
a wrong side row.

**Shape neck**

**Next row** (right side) Patt to last 9(10:11:12) sts,
leave these sts on a holder, turn and work on
rem 37(40:43:46) sts.
Dec one st at neck edge on every row until
27(30:32:35) sts rem.
Cont straight until front measures same as Back

to shoulder shaping, ending at armhole edge.

**Shape shoulder**

Cast off 13(15:16:17) sts at beg of next row.

Work 1 row.

Cast off rem 14(15:16:18) sts.

Mark positions for 3(3:4:4) buttons the first on
the 3rd row of rib patt, the 3rd(3rd:4th:4th) 1cm
below neck shaping with the rem 1(1:2:2)
spaced evenly between.


RIGHT FRONT

With 3.75mm needles, cast on 53(59:65:71) sts.

K 3 rows.

Change to 4mm needles.

**Next row** (right side) K to end.

**Next row** P to last 3 sts, k3.

These 2 rows form the st st with garter st border.

Cont straight until front measures
34(36:39:42)cm in from cast on edge, ending
with a wrong side row.

**1st and 3rd sizes only**

**Next row** (right side) K5, * p2, k2; rep from
* to end.

**Next row** P2, * k2, p2; rep from * to last
3 sts, k3.

**2nd and 4th sizes only**

**Next row** (right side) K5, p2, * k2, p2; rep from
* to end.

**Next row** K2, * p2, k2; rep from * to last 5 sts,
p2, k3.

**All sizes**

These 2 rows form the rib patt with garter
st border.

**Next row** (right side buttonhole row) K2, yf,
k2tog, k1, rib to end.

Work rem buttonholes as set by this row to
match button markers.

Cont straight until front measures 38(41:45:49)cm from cast on edge, ending with a right side row.

### Shape armhole

Cast off 7(9:11:13) sts at beg of next row. 46(50:54:58) sts.

Cont straight until front measures 49(53:57:63)cm from cast on edge, ending with a wrong side row.

### Shape neck

**Next row** (right side) Patt 9(10:11:12) sts and leave these sts on a holder, patt to end. 37(40:43:46) sts.

Dec one st at neck edge on every row until 27(30:32:35) sts rem.

Cont straight until front measures same as Back to shoulder shaping, ending at armhole edge.

### Shape shoulder

Cast off 13(15:16:17) sts at beg of next row.

Work 1 row.

Cast off rem 14(15:16:18) sts.

### SLEEVES

With 3.75mm needles, cast on 50(54:58:62) sts.

**1st row** (right side) K2, * p2, k2; rep from * to end.

**2nd row** P2, * k2, p2; rep from * to end.

These 2 rows form the rib patt.

Work a further 4(6:8:10) rows.

Change to 4mm needles.

Cont in rib.

Inc one st at each end of the 3rd and every foll 4th row until there are 88(96:102:114) sts.

Cont straight until sleeve measures 31(35:39:43)cm from cast on edge, ending with a wrong side row.

Place a marker at each end of last row.

Work a further 6(8:10:12) rows.

Cast off.

### COLLAR

Join shoulder seams.

With right side facing and 3.75mm needles, slip 9(10:11:12) sts from right front neck holder onto a needle, pick up and k18(18:19:21) sts up right front neck, 34(36:40:42) sts across back neck, 18(18:19:21) sts down left front neck, then patt 9(10:11:12) sts from left front holder. 88(92:100:108) sts.

**1st rib row** (wrong side) K3, * p2, k2; rep from * to last 5 sts, p2, k3.

**2nd rib row** K5, * p2, k2; rep from * to last 7 sts, p2, k5.

**3rd and 4th sizes only**

**Next 2 rows** Rib to last 29 sts, turn.

**All sizes**

**Next 2 rows** Rib to last 25 sts, turn.

**Next 2 rows** Rib to last 21 sts, turn.

**Next 2 rows** Rib to last 17 sts, turn.

**Next 2 rows** Rib to last 13 sts, turn.

**Next 2 rows** Rib to last 9 sts, turn.

**Next row** Rib to end.

Change to 4mm needles.

Cont in rib across all sts for a further 7(7:8:9)cm.

Cast off in rib.

### TIE

With 3.75mm needles, cast on 6 sts.

Cont in garter st until tie measures 150cm from cast on edge.

Cast off.

### TO MAKE UP

With centre of sleeves to shoulder seam, sew sleeves into armholes with row ends above markers sewn to sts cast off at underarm.

Join side and sleeve seams. Make belt loops on side seams over first 4 rows of ribbed yoke. Sew on buttons.

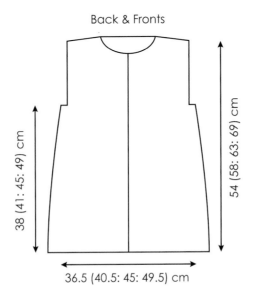

Back & Fronts

38 (41: 45: 49) cm

54 (58: 63: 69) cm

36.5 (40.5: 45: 49.5) cm

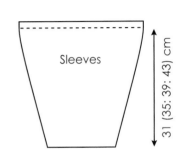

Sleeves

31 (35: 39: 43) cm

# sun hat

**SIZES**

To fit ages          1–2 years

**MATERIALS**

Two 50g balls of Debbie Bliss cathay in Lime
Pair of 3.75mm knitting needles.

**TENSION**

22 sts and 30 rows to 10cm square over st st
using 3.75mm needles.

**ABBREVIATIONS**

beg = beginning; cont = continue; cm =
centimetre; dec = decrease; k = knit;
m1 = make one st by picking up and working
into back of loop lying between st just worked
and next st; p = purl; patt = pattern;
rem = remaining; st(s) = stitch(es);
st st = stocking stitch; tog = together;
yf = yarn forward.

**MAIN HAT**

With 3.75mm needles, cast on 94 sts.

Beg with a k row, work 9cm in st st, ending with
a p row and dec 3 sts evenly across last row. 91
sts.

**Shape top**

**Dec row** [K8, k2tog] to last st, k1.

P 1 row.

**Dec row** [K7, k2tog] to last st, k1.

P 1 row.

**Dec row** [K6, k2tog] to last st, k1.

Cont in this way and dec 9 sts on every right
side row until 19 sts rem.

P 1 row.

**Dec row** [K2tog] to last st, k1.

Break yarn, thread through rem 10 sts, pull up
and secure.

**BRIM**

With right side facing and 3.75mm needles,
pick up and k92 sts evenly along cast on edge
of main hat.

Beg with a p row, work in st st.

Work 1 row.

**1st inc row** K1, [m1, k6, m1, k7] 7 times.

Work 2 rows.

**2nd inc row** [P8, m1, p7, m1] 7 times, p1.

Work 2 rows.

**3rd inc row** K1, [m1, k8, m1, k9] 7 times.

Work 2 rows.

**4th inc row** [P10, m1, p9, m1] 7 times, p1.

148 sts.

K 1 row.

Cast off.

**EDGING**

With 3.75mm needles, cast on 4 sts.

**1st row** (wrong side) K2, yf, k2.

**2nd, 4th and 6th rows** K.

**3rd row** K3, yf, k2.

**5th row** K2, yf, k2tog, yf, k2.

**7th row** K3, yf, k2tog, yf, k2.

**8th row** Cast off 4, k to end.

These 8 rows form the patt and are repeated.

Cont in patt until edging fits around edge of
brim, ending with a 7th row.

Cast off.

Sew edging to brim.

Join seam.

# rib and cable cardigan

## MEASUREMENTS

To fit bust

86–91     97–102cm

Finished measurements

Bust

94          107cm

Length to shoulder

54          58cm

Sleeve length

46cm for both sizes

## MATERIALS

10(11) 50g balls of Debbie Bliss cashmerino dk
in Apple Green

Pair of 3.75mm knitting needles

Cable needle

10 buttons

## TENSION

24 sts and 30 rows to 10cm square over rib,
when lightly pressed, using 3.75mm needles.

## ABBREVIATIONS

beg = beginning; C4B = slip next 2 sts onto cable
needle, hold at back of work, k2, then k2 from
cable needle; C4F = slip next 2 sts onto cable
needle, hold to front of work, k2, then k2 from
cable needle; cm = centimetre; cont = continue;
dec = decrease; foll = following; inc = increase;
k = knit; kfb = k into front and back of st;
kfpb = k into front of st and purl into back of st;
p = purl; pfb = purl into front and back of st;
pfkb = purl into front and knit into back of st;
skpo = slip one, k1, pass slip st over;
st(s) = stitch(es); st st = stocking st; tog = together;
yf = yarn forward to make a st.

## BACK

With 3.75mm needles, cast on 158(182) sts.

**1st row** (right side) K3, [p8, k4] 12(14) times,
p8, k3.

**2nd row** P3, [k8, p4] 12(14) times, k8, p3.

These 2 rows form wide rib.

Rib 9 more rows.

**1st dec row** (wrong side) P3, [skpo, k4, k2tog,
p4] 12(14) times, skpo, k4, k2tog, p3.
132(152) sts.

**Next row** (right side) K3, [p6, k4] 12(14) times,
p6, k3.

Cont in rib as set, work 6 more rows.

**2nd dec row** (wrong side) P3, [skpo, k2, k2tog,
p4] 12(14) times, skpo, k2, k2tog, p3.
106(122) sts.

**Next row** K3, [p4, k4] to last 7 sts, p4, k3.

Cont in rib as set, work 3 rows.

**Shape waist**

**1st row** (right side) K3, p4, k4, [p4, C4B] 5(6)
times, p4, [C4F, p4] 5(6) times, k4, p4, k3.

Rib 3 rows.

Work the last 4 rows 4 more times, then work
1st row again.

Cont in rib, work 3(5) rows.

**Inc row** (right side) K1, kfb, rib to last 3 sts, kfb,
k2. 108(124) sts.

Taking inc sts into st st, cont in rib, inc in this
way at each end of 3 foll 10th rows.
114(130) sts.

Work 21(23) rows straight.

**Shape armholes** Cast off 4 sts at beg of next
2 rows. 106(122) sts.

**Dec row** (right side) K2, skpo, rib to last 4 sts,

k2tog, k2. 104(120) sts.

Cont in rib, dec in this way at each end of next
5 right side rows. 94(110) sts.

Rib 47(57) rows.

Cast off.

## LEFT FRONT

With 3.75mm needles, cast on 80(92) sts.

**1st row** (right side) K3, [p8, k4] 6(7) times, k5.

**2nd row** k5, [p4, k8] 6(7) times, p3.

These 2 rows form wide rib with k5 at front edge
on every row for buttonband.

Work 9 more rows.

**1st dec row** (wrong side) K5, [p4, skpo, k4,
k2tog] 6(7) times, p3. 68(78) sts.

**Next row** K3, [p6, k4] 6(7) times, k5.

Cont in rib as set with k5 band, work 6 rows.

**2nd dec row** (wrong side) K5, [p4, skpo, k2,
k2tog] 6(7) times, p3. 56(64) sts.

**Next row** (right side) K3, [p4, k4] 6(7) times, k5.

Cont as set, work 3 rows.

**Shape waist**

**1st row** (right side) K3, p4, k4, [p4, C4B] 5(6)
times, k5.

Work 3 rows rib with k5 band.

Work the last 4 rows 4 more times, then work
1st row again.

Work 3(5) rows.

**Inc row** (right side) K1, kfb, rib to last 5 sts, k5.
57(65) sts.

Taking incs into st st, inc in this way at beg of 3
foll 10th rows. 60(68) sts.

Work 21(23) rows straight.

## Shape armhole

Cast off 4 sts at beg of next row. 56(64) sts.

Work 1 row.

**Dec row** (right side) K2, skpo, rib to last 5 sts, k5. 55(63) sts.

Dec in this way at beg of next 5 right side rows. 50(58) sts.

Work 25(35) rows.

## Shape neck

**Next row** (right side) Rib 40(48), turn and leave 10 sts on a holder for neck.

[Cast off 2 sts at beg of next row and dec one st at end of foll row] 6 times. 22(30) sts.

Rib 9 rows.

Cast off.

Mark positions for 9 buttons, the top one 3cm down from neck edge with 8 more spaced 14(16) rows apart. The 10th buttonhole will be in the collar.

## RIGHT FRONT

Make buttonholes opposite markers when appropriate as follows:

**Buttonhole row** (right side) K2, yf, k2tog, k1, patt to end.

With 3.75mm needles, cast on 80(92) sts.

**1st row** (right side) K5, [k4, p8] 6(7) times, k3.

**2nd row** P3, [k8, p4] 6(7) times, k5.

These 2 rows form wide rib with k5 at front edge on every row for buttonhole band.

Work 9 more rows.

**1st dec row** (wrong side) P3, [skpo, k4, k2tog, p4] 6(7) times, k5. 68(78) sts.

**Next row** K5, [k4, p6] 6(7) times, k3.

Cont in rib as set work 6 rows.

**2nd dec row** (wrong side) P3, [skpo, k2, k2tog, p4] 6(7) times, k5. 56(64) sts.

**Next row** (right side) K5, [k4, p4] 6(7) times, k3.

Cont as set, work 3 rows.

## Shape waist

**1st row** (right side) K5, [C4F, p4] 5(6) times, k4, p4, k3.

Work 3 rows rib with k5 front band.

Work the last 4 rows 4 times more, then work 1st row again.

Rib 3(5) rows.

**Inc row** (right side) K5, rib to last 3 sts, kfb, k2. 57(65) sts.

Taking incs into st st, inc in this way at end of 3 foll 10th rows. 60(68) sts.

Work 22(24) rows.

## Shape armhole

Cast off 4 sts at beg of next row. 56(64) sts.

**Dec row** (right side) K5, rib to last 4 sts, k2tog, k2. 55(63) sts.

Dec in this way at end of next 5 right side rows. 50(58) sts.

Work 25(35) rows.

## Shape neck

**Next row** (right side) K5, rib 5 and leave these 10 sts on a holder for neckband, rib to end. 40(48) sts.

[Dec one st at end of next row and cast off 2 sts at beg of foll row] 6 times. 22(30) sts.

Rib 9 rows.

Cast off.

## SLEEVES

With 3.75mm needles, cast on 72(92) sts.

**1st row** (right side) K3, [p6, k4] 6(8) times, p6, k3.

**2nd row** P3, [k6, p4] 6(8) times, k6, p3.

These 2 rows form wide rib for cuff.

Rib 5 more rows.

**Dec row** (wrong side) P3, [skpo, k2, k2tog, p4] 6(8) times, skpo, k2, k2tog, p3. 58(74) sts.

Cont in rib, work 2 rows.

Work cable band.

**1st row** (right side) K3, [p4, C4B] 3(4) times, p4, [C4F, p4] 3(4) times, k3.

**2nd and 4th rows** P3, [k4, p4] to last 7 sts, k4, p3.

**3rd row** K3, [p4, k4] to last 7 sts, p4, k3.

These 4 rows form the cable patt.

Work the last 4 rows once more, then work 1st row again.

Cont in rib, work 11 rows.

Keeping 1 st at each end of every right side row as k1 and every wrong side row as p1, work incs as follows:

**1st inc row** (right side) Kfb, rib to last 2 sts, kfb, k1. 60(76) sts.

Taking inc sts into knit rib, inc in this way at each end of foll 8th row. 62(78) sts.

Work 7 rows.

**3rd inc row** Kfpb, rib to last 2 sts, kfpb, k1. 64(80) sts.

Working inc sts in purl rib, work 7 rows.

**4th inc row** (right side) Kfpb, rib to last 2 sts, pfb, k1. 66(82) sts.

Taking inc sts into purl rib, inc in same way as 4th inc row at each end of 2 foll 8th rows. 70(86) sts.

**7th inc row** Kfb, rib to last 2 sts, pfkb, k1. 72(88) sts.

Work 7 rows.

Taking all inc sts into knit rib, inc in same way as 1st inc row on next row and 4 foll 8th rows. 82(98) sts.

Work 19 rows.

**Shape top**

Cast off 4 sts at beg of next 2 rows. 74(90) sts.

**Dec row** (right side) K2, skpo, rib to last 4 sts, k2tog, k2.

Cont in rib, dec in this way at each end of next 5 right side rows. 62(78) sts.

Work 1 row.

Cast off 2 sts at beg and dec one st at end of next 10 rows. 32(48) sts.

Cast off.

## COLLAR

Join shoulder seams. With right side facing, and 3.75mm needles, slip 10 sts from right front holder onto needle, join on yarn and pick up and k26 sts up right front neck, 52 sts evenly across back neck edge and 26 sts down left front neck, then k10 from left front holder. 124 sts.

K 1 row.

**Dec row** K36, [k2tog, k2] 6 times, k2tog, skpo, [k2, skpo] 6 times, k36. 110 sts.

K 3 rows.

**Next row** K2, yf, k2tog, k to end.

K 1 row.

**Next row** Cast off 4 sts purlwise, k to end.

**Next row** Cast off 4 sts knitwise, k to end. 102 sts.

**Inc row** K31, [kfb, k2] 6 times, [kfb] twice, k1, [k2, kfb] 6 times, k32. 116 sts.

Now work in rib as follows:

**1st row** (right side of collar) K8, [p4, k4] to last 4 sts, k4.

**2nd row** K4, [p4, k4] to end.

These 2 rows form rib with k4 at each end on every row.

Cont until collar measures 6cm from 1st row of rib, ending with a right side row.

Cast off knitwise.

## TO MAKE UP

Press very lightly according to ball band. Sew sleeves into armholes. Join side and sleeve seams. Sew on buttons.

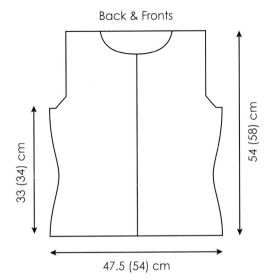

Back & Fronts

33 (34) cm

54 (58) cm

47.5 (54) cm

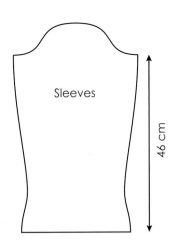

Sleeves

46 cm

# cricket sweater

## MEASUREMENTS

To fit chest

92–97    102–107  112–117  122–127cm

Finished measurements

Chest

112      125      134      146cm

Length to shoulder

66       68       70       72cm

Sleeve length

54       54       55       55cm

## MATERIALS

15(17:18:20) 50g balls of Debbie Bliss extra fine merino dk in Pale Blue (A) and two 50g balls in Chocolate (B)

Pair each size 3.75mm and 4mm knitting needles

Circular 3.25mm needle

Cable needle

## TENSION

26 sts and 31 rows to 10cm square over patt when slightly stretched using 4mm needles.

## ABBREVIATIONS

alt = alternate; beg = beginning; C6F = slip next 3 sts onto cable needle and hold at front of work, k3, then k3 from cable needle; cm = centimetre; cont = continue; dec = decrease; foll = following; inc = increase; k = knit; m1 = make one st by picking up and working into back of loop lying between st just worked and next st; p = purl; patt = pattern; rem = remaining; rep = repeat; st(s) = stitch(es); st st = stocking stitch; tbl = through back loop; tog = together.

## BACK

With 3.75mm needles and B, cast on 128(140:152:164) sts.

**1st rib row** P2, * k4, p2; rep from * to end.

**2nd rib row** K2, * p4, k2; rep from * to end.

These 2 rows form the rib patt.

Work 4 rows A, 4 rows B and 2 rows A, 1 row B.

**Inc row** (wrong side) With B, rib 9(3:9:3), [m1, rib 2, m1, rib 10] 9(11:11:13) times, m1, rib 2, m1, rib 9(3:9:3).

148(164:176:192) sts.

Change to 4mm needles and A.

**1st row** (right side) [P2, k4] 1(0:1:0) times, [p2, k6, p2, k4] 9(11:11:13) times, p2, k6, p2, [k4, p2] 1(0:1:0) times.

**2nd row** [K2, p4] 1(0:1:0) times, [k2, p6, k2, p4] 9(11:11:13) times, k2, p6, k2, [p4, k2] 1(0:1:0) times.

**3rd and 4th rows** As 1st and 2nd rows.

**5th row** [P2, k4] 1(0:1:0) times, [p2, C6F, p2, k4] 9(11:11:13) times, p2, C6F, p2, [k4, p2] 1(0:1:0) times.

**6th row** As 2nd row.

**7th to 12 rows** Rep 1st and 2nd rows three times more.

These 12 rows form the patt and are repeated throughout.

Cont in patt until back measures 40(41:42:43)cm from cast on edge, ending with wrong side row.

### Shape armholes

Cast off 6(8:6:8) sts at beg of next 2 rows. 136(148:164:176) sts.**

Cont straight until back measures

61(63:65:67)cm from cast on edge, ending with a wrong side row.

### Shape neck

**Next row** Patt 50(56:58:64), turn and work on these sts for first side of neck shaping.

Dec one st at neck edge on the next 5(7:5:5) rows. 45(49:53:59) sts.

Cont straight until back measures 66(68:70:72)cm from cast on edge, ending at armhole edge.

### Shape shoulders

Cast off 15(16:18:20) sts at beg of next row and foll alt row.

Work 1 row.

Cast off rem 15(17:17:19) sts.

With right side facing, slip next 36(36:48:48) sts on a holder, rejoin yarn A to rem sts, patt to end.

Complete to match first side.

## FRONT

Work as given for Back to **. 136(148:164:176) sts.

### Shape neck

**Next row** Patt 64(70:78:84), work 2tog, turn and work on these sts for first side of neck shaping.

Dec one st at neck edge on 10(11:12:13) foll alt rows then on every foll 4th row until 45(49:53:59) sts rem.

Cont straight until front measures the same as Back to shoulder, ending at armhole edge.

### Shape shoulder

**Next row** Cast off 15(16:18:20) sts at beg of next and foll alt row.

Work 1 row.

Cast off rem 15(17:17:19) sts.

With right side facing, slip centre 4 sts onto a safety pin, rejoin yarn to rem sts, work 2 tog, patt to end.

Complete to match first side, reversing shaping.

## SLEEVES

With 3.75mm needles and B, cast on 56(56:68:68) sts.

**1st rib row** P2, * k4, p2; rep from * to end.

**2nd rib row** K2, * p4, k2; rep from * to end.

These 2 rows form the rib patt.

Work 4 rows A, 4 rows B and 2 rows A, 1 row B.

**Inc row** (wrong side) Rib 3, [m1, rib 2, m1, rib 10] 4(4:5:5) times, m1, rib 2, m1, rib 3. 66(66:80:80) sts.

Change to 4mm needles.

**1st row** (right side) [P2, k6, p2, k4] 4(4:5:5) times, p2, k6, p2.

**2nd row** [K2, p6, k2, p4] 4(4:5:5) times, k2, p6, k2.

**3rd and 4th rows** As 1st and 2nd rows.

**5th row** [P2, C6F, p2, k4] 4(4:5:5) times, p2, C6F, p2.

**6th row** As 2nd row.

These 6 rows **set** the position of the 12 row patt.

Keeping patt correct, inc one st at each end of the next row and every foll 4th row until there are 94(106:96:110) sts, then on every foll 6th row until there are 120(126:132:138) sts, working inc sts into patt.

Work straight until sleeve measures 54(54:55:55)cm from cast on edge, ending with a wrong side row.

Place markers at each end of last row.

Work a further 4(6:4:6) rows.

Cast off 10 sts at beg of next 8 rows.

Cast off rem 40(46:52:58) sts.

## NECKBAND

Join right shoulder seam.

With right side facing, 3.25mm circular needle and A, pick up and k68(68:74:74) sts down left front neck, k4 sts from safety pin at centre front and mark centre 2 sts of these 4, pick up and k66(66:72:72) sts up right front neck, 18 sts down right back neck, then patt across 36(36:48:48) sts at back neck decreasing 2 sts across each cable, pick up and k18 sts up left back neck. 206(206:230:230) sts.

Work backwards and forwards in rows.

**1st rib row** K2, * p4, k2; rep from * to end.

Change to B.

**2nd rib row** (dec row) Rib to within 2 sts of marker, k2tog, k2, k2tog tbl, rib to end.

**3rd rib row** Rib to end.

The last 2 rows form the rib and are repeated.

Work 2 rows A, 4 rows B, 4 rows A, 4 rows B.

With B, cast off in rib, decreasing on this row as before.

## TO MAKE UP

Join left shoulder and neckband seam. Join side and sleeve seams. Sew sleeves into armholes.

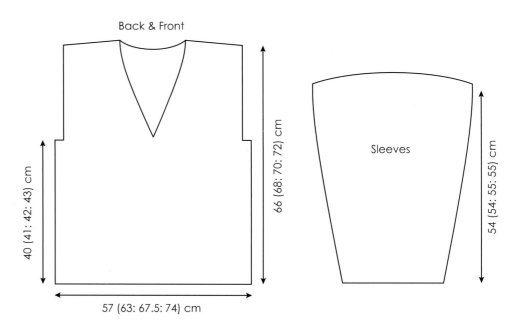

Back & Front

40 (41: 42: 43) cm

66 (68: 70: 72) cm

57 (63: 67.5: 74) cm

Sleeves

54 (54: 55: 55) cm

# fair isle cardigan

## MEASUREMENTS

To fit ages

| 1–2 | 2–3 | 3–4 | 4–5 years |
|-----|-----|-----|-----------|

Finished measurements

Chest

| 57 | 62 | 67 | 71cm |
|----|----|----|------|

Length to shoulder

| 28 | 31 | 34 | 37cm |
|----|----|----|------|

Sleeve length

| 19 | 22 | 25 | 28cm |
|----|----|----|------|

## MATERIALS

3(3:3:3) 50g balls of Debbie Bliss baby
cashmerino in Pale Pink (A) and one 50g ball in
each of Deep Pink (B), Teal (C), Pale Blue (D),
Ecru (E) and Lime (F)
Pair of each size 3mm and 3.25mm knitting
needles
3 buttons

## TENSION

25 sts and 34 rows to 10cm square over st st
using 3.25mm needles.

## ABBREVIATIONS

alt = alternate; beg = beginning;
cm = centimetre; cont = continue;
dec = decrease; foll = following; inc = increase;
k = knit; p = purl; patt = pattern;
rem = remaining; rep = repeat; st(s) = stitch(es);
st st = stocking stitch; tog = together; yo = yarn
over needle.

## BACK

With 3mm needles and B, cast on 71(77:83:89)
sts.
Change to A.
**Moss st row** K1, * p1, k1; rep from * to end.
This row forms moss st.
Rep this row 5 times more.
Change to 3.25mm needles.
Beg with a k row work in st st .
Work 6 rows.
Now work in patt as follows:
Work 13 rows from Chart 1.
With A, beg with a p row, work 5 rows in st st.
Work 13 rows from Chart 2.
With A, beg with a p row, work 5 rows st st.
The last 36 rows form the patt and are repeated.
Cont in patt until back measures
17(19:21:23)cm from cast on edge, ending with
a p row.
### Shape armholes
Cast off 4 sts at beg of next 2 rows.
63(69:75:81) sts.
Dec one st at each end of the next row and
2(3:4:5) foll alt rows. 57(61:65:69) sts.
Cont straight until back measures
28(31:34:37)cm from cast on edge, ending with
a p row.
### Shape shoulders
Cast off 10(11:12:13) sts at beg of next 2 rows.
Leave rem 37(39:41:43) sts on a holder.

## LEFT FRONT

With 3mm needles and B, cast on 40(43:46:49)
sts.

Change to A.

**1st moss st row** (right side) K0(1:0:1), * p1, k1; rep from * to end.

**2nd moss st row** * K1, p1; rep from * to last 0(1:0:1) st, k0(1:0:1).

Rep these 2 rows twice more.

Change to 3.25mm needles.

**1st row** K to last 4 sts, [p1, k1] twice.

**2nd row** K1, p1, k1, p to end.

These 2 rows form the st st with moss st border.

Work 4 more rows.

**7th row** Work in patt from Chart 1 to last 4 sts, with A [p1, k1] twice.

**8th row** With A, [k1, p1] twice, work in patt from Chart 1 to end.

These 2 rows **set** the patt.

Cont in patt to end of Chart 1.

With A, work 5 rows in st st with moss st border.

Work 13 rows from Chart 2, with moss st border.

With A, work 5 rows in st st with moss st border.

The last 36 rows form the patt and are repeated.

Cont straight until front measures 17(19:21:23)cm from cast on edge, ending with a wrong side row.

**Shape armhole**

Cast off 4 sts at beg of next row. 36(39:42:45) sts.

Work 1 row.

Dec one st at armhole edge of the next and 2(3:4:5) foll alt rows. 33(35:37:39) sts.

Cont straight until front measures 21(24:26:29)cm from cast on edge, ending with a wrong side row.

**Shape neck**

**Next row** Patt to last 8(9:10:11) sts, leave these sts on a holder.

Dec one st at neck edge on every row until 10(11:12:13) sts rem.

Cont straight until front measures same as Back to shoulder, ending at armhole edge.

**Shape shoulder**

Cast off.

Mark positions for two buttons, the first 4cm below neck edge, the second 9cm below neck edge.


RIGHT FRONT

Work buttonholes to match button positions as follows:

**Buttonhole row** (right side) K1, p1, yo, p2tog, patt to end.

With 3mm needles and B, cast on 40(43:46:49) sts.

Change to A.

**1st moss st row** (right side) K1, * p1, k1; rep from * to last 1(0:1:0) st, p1(0:1:0).

**2nd moss st row** P1(0:1:0), k1, * p1, k1; rep from * to end.

Rep these 2 rows twice more.

Change to 3.25mm needles.

**1st row** [K1, p1] twice, k to end.

**2nd row** P to last 3 sts, k1, p1, k1.

These 2 rows form the st st with moss st border.

Work 4 more rows.

**7th row** With A [k1, p1] twice, work in patt from Chart 1 to end.

**8th row** Work in patt from Chart 1 to last 4 sts, with A [p1, k1] twice.

These 2 rows **set** the patt.

Cont in patt to end of Chart 1.

With A, work 5 rows in st st with moss st border.

Work 13 rows from Chart 2, with moss st border.

With A, work 5 rows in st st with moss st border.

The last 36 rows form the patt and are repeated.

Cont straight until front measures

17(19:21:23)cm from cast on edge, ending with a right side row.

**Shape armhole**

Cast off 4 sts at beg of next row. 36(39:42:45) sts.

Dec one st at armhole edge of the next row and 2(3:4:5) foll alt rows. 33(35:37:39) sts.

Cont straight until front measures 21(24:26:29)cm from cast on edge, ending with a wrong side row.

**Shape neck**

**Next row** Patt 8(9:10:11) sts, leave these sts on a holder, patt to end.

Dec one st at neck edge on every row until 10(11:12:13) sts rem.

Cont straight until front measures same as Back to shoulder, ending at armhole edge.

**Shape shoulder**

Cast off.


SLEEVES

With 3mm needles and B, cast on 37(39:43:45) sts.

Change to A.

**Moss st row** K1, * p1, k1; rep from * to end.

Rep this row 5 times more.

Change to 3.25mm needles.

Beg with a k row, work 6 rows in st st, inc one st at each end of the 5th row. 39(41:45:47) sts.

Work 4 rows in patt from Chart 1 setting the position as follows: work 3(4:6:7) sts at beg of right side rows and end of wrong side rows, work 16 st patt rep twice, work 4(5:7:8) sts at end of right side rows and beg of wrong side rows all inc sts should be worked into chart patt.

Cont in patt from Chart 1, inc one st at end of the next and foll 6th row.

Work last 2 rows of Chart 1.

With A, work 5 rows in st st and inc one st at each end of the 4th row.

Cont in patt from Chart 2, inc one st at each end of the 5th and foll 6th rows.

With A, work 5 rows in st st and inc one st at each end of the 4th row.

These 36 rows **set** the position of the charts.

Cont in patt and inc and work into patt one st at each end of every foll 4th row until there are 55(61:67:73) sts.

Cont straight until sleeve measures 19(22:25:28)cm from cast on edge, ending with a p row.

**Shape top**

Cast off 4 sts at beg of next 2 rows. 47(53:59:65) sts.

Dec one st at each end of the next row and 2(3:4:5) foll alt rows. 41(45:49:53) sts.

Cast off.

NECKBAND

With right side facing, 3.25mm needles and A, slip 8(9:10:11) sts from right front holder onto a needle, pick up and k24(24:26:26) sts up right front neck, k37(39:41:43) sts from back neck holder, pick up and k24(24:26:26) sts down left front neck, then k8(9:10:11) sts from left front holder. 101(105:113:117) sts.

Work in moss st as set by front band sts.

Work 1 row.

**Buttonhole row** (right side) K1, p1, yo, p2tog, moss st to end.

Change to 3mm needles.

Moss st 3 rows.

With B, cast off in moss st.

TO MAKE UP

Sew sleeves into armholes. Join side and sleeve seams. Sew on buttons.

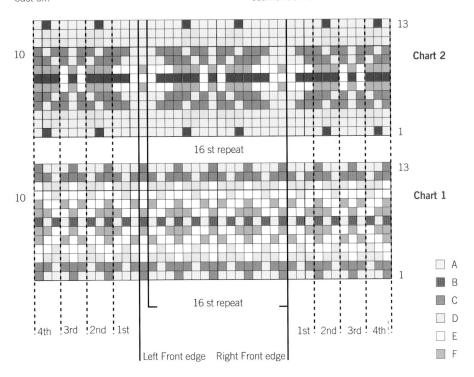

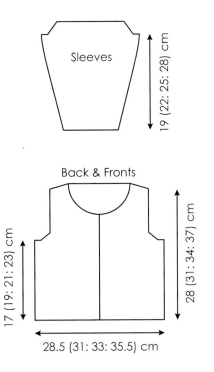

Chart 2

13

10

1

16 st repeat

Chart 1

13

10

1

16 st repeat

4th  3rd  2nd  1st        1st  2nd  3rd  4th

Left Front edge    Right Front edge

A
B
C
D
E
F

Sleeves

19 (22: 25: 28) cm

Back & Fronts

17 (19: 21: 23) cm

28 (31: 34: 37) cm

28.5 (31: 33: 35.5) cm

# skinny rib cardigan

## MEASUREMENTS

To fit bust

76–82    87–92    97–102    107–112cm

Finished measurements with rib stretched

to fit

Bust

82        92        103        112cm

Length to back neck

47        51        55        59cm

Sleeve length

45        46        48        48cm

## MATERIALS

8(9:10:11) 50g balls of Debbie Bliss cathay in
Teal (A) and one 50g ball in Lime (B)
Pair of 3.75mm knitting needles
One 3.25mm circular needle
12 small buttons

## TENSION

30 sts and 30 rows to 10cm square over rib patt
when left unstretched and 23 sts and 33 rows to
10cm square over rib patt when stretched, both
using 3.75mm needles.

## ABBREVIATIONS

beg = beginning; cont = continue;
cm = centimetre; dec = decrease;
foll = following; inc = increase; k = knit;
p = purl; patt = pattern; rem = remaining;
rep = repeat; skpo = sl 1, k1, pass slipped st
over; sl = slip; st(s) = stitch(es); st st = stocking
stitch; tog = together; yf = yarn forward.

## BACK

With 3.75mm needles and B, cast on
95(104:116:128) sts.

**1st row** (right side) P2, [k1, p2] to end.

**2nd row** K2, [p1, k2] to end.

Rep the last 2 rows 3 times more.

Change to A and k 1 row.

**Next row** (wrong side) K2, [p1, k2] to end.

**Next row** (right side) P2, [k1, p2] to end.

Cont in patt as set and work a further
79(85:91:97) rows, so ending with a wrong
side row.

### Shape underarm and raglan

Cast off 3 sts in patt at beg of next 2 rows.
89(98:110:122) sts.

**Next row** P2, skpo, patt to last 4 sts, k2tog, p2.

**Next row** K2, p1, patt to last 3 sts, p1, k2.

Rep the last 2 rows 15(18:21:24) times more.
57(60:66:72) sts.

**Next row** P2, k1, patt to last 3 sts, k1, p2.

**Next row** K2, p1, patt to last 3 sts, p1, k2.

**Next row** P2, skpo, patt to last 4 sts, k2tog, p2.

**Next row** K2, p1, patt to last 3 sts, p1, k2.

Rep the last 4 rows once more. 53(56:62:68) sts.
Leave all sts on a holder.

## LEFT FRONT

With 3.75mm needles and B, cast on
52(58:64:70) sts.

**1st row** (right side) P2, [k1, p2] to last 5 sts, k2,
p1, k2.

**2nd row** P2, k1, p2, [k2, p1] to last 2 sts, k2.

These 2 rows form the rib patt with 5-st front
buttonband and are repeated 3 times more.

Change to A and k 1 row.

Beg with a 2nd row, work a further 81(87:93:99)
rows in patt, so ending with a wrong side row.

### Shape underarm and raglan

**Next row** Cast off 3 sts, patt to end.
49(55:61:67) sts.

Patt 1 row.

**Next row** P2, skpo, patt to end.

**Next row** Patt to last 3 sts, p1, k2.

Rep the last 2 rows 15(18:21:24) times more.
33(36:39:42) sts.

**Next row** P2, k1, patt to end.

**Next row** Patt to last 3 sts, p1, k2.

**Next row** P2, skpo, patt to end.

**Next row** Patt to last 3 sts, p1, k2.

Rep the last 4 rows once more. 31(34:37:40) sts.
Leave all sts on a holder.

Mark the position for 11 buttons, the first to be
worked on the 3rd row after cast on, the 12th
will be worked on the 4th row of the neckband,
with the others spaced evenly between.

## RIGHT FRONT

**Buttonhole row** (right side) K2, yf, k2tog, k1,
patt to end.

With 3.75mm needles, cast on 52(58:64:70) sts.

**1st row** (right side) K2, p1, k2, [p2, k1] to last
2 sts, p2.

**2nd row** K2, [p1, k2] to last 5 sts, p2, k1, p2.

These 2 rows form the rib patt with 5-st front
buttonhole band and are repeated.

**3rd row** (buttonhole row) K2, yf, k2tog, k1, patt
to end.

Work a further 5 rows in patt.

Change to A and k1 row.

Cont in patt for a further 82(88:94:100) rows, so ending with a right side row, working buttonholes to match markers.

**Shape underarm and raglan**

**Next row** (wrong side) Cast off 3 sts, patt to end. 49(55:61:67) sts.

Cont to work buttonholes and shape as follows:

**Next row** Patt to last 4 sts, k2tog, p2.

**Next row** K2, p1, patt to end.

Rep the last 2 rows 15(18:21:24) times more. 33(36:39:42) sts.

**Next row** Patt to last 3 sts, k1, p2.

**Next row** K2, p1, patt to end.

**Next row** Patt to last 4 sts, k2tog, p2.

**Next row** K2, p1, patt to end.

Rep the last 4 rows once more. 31(34:37:40) sts.

Leave all sts on a holder.

## SLEEVES

With 3.75mm needles and B, cast on 47(47:53:59) sts.

**1st row** (right side) P2, [k1, p2] to end.

**2nd row** K2, [p1, k2] to end.

These 2 rows form the rib patt and are repeated.

Work 6 rows.

Change to A and k 1 row.

Beg with a 2nd row, cont in patt and inc 1 st at each end of 6th(8th:10th:10th) row and every foll 8th(7th:7th:7th) row until there are 77(83:89:95) sts.

Cont straight until sleeve measures 45(46:48:48)cm from cast on edge, ending with a wrong side row.

**Shape underarm and raglan**

Cast off 3 sts in patt at beg of next 2 rows.

71(77:83:89) sts.

**Next row** P2, skpo, patt to last 4 sts, k2tog, p2.

**Next row** K2, p1, patt to last 3 sts, p1, k2.

Rep the last 2 rows 15(18:21:24) times more. 39 sts.

**Next row** P2, k1, patt to last 3 sts, k1, p2.

**Next row** K2, p1, patt to last 3 sts, p1, k2.

**Next row** P2, skpo, patt to last 4 sts, k2tog, p2.

**Next row** K2, p1, patt to last 3 sts, p1, k2.

Rep the last 4 rows once more. 35 sts.

Leave all sts on a holder.

## NECKBAND

With right side facing, 3.25mm circular needle and A, patt across right front to last st, p last st tog with first st of right sleeve, patt to last st, p last st tog with first st of back, patt to last st, p last st tog with first st of left sleeve, patt to last st, p last st tog with first st of left front, patt to end. 181(190:202:214) sts.

**Dec row** (wrong side) P2, k1, p2, [k2, p1] 8(9:10:11) times, k2tog, k1, p1, [k2, p1] 10 times, k2tog, k1, p1, [k2, p1] 16(17:19:21) times, k2tog, k1, p1, [k2, p1] 10 times, k2tog, k1, [p1, k2] 8(9:10:11) times, p2, k1, p2. 177(186:198:210) sts.

**2nd row** K2, p1, k2, [p2, k1] to last 7 sts, p2, k2, p1, k2.

**3rd row** P2, k1, p2, [k2, p1] to last 7 sts, k2, p2, k1, p2.

**4th row** (buttonhole row) K2, yf, k2tog, k1, [p2, k1] to last 7 sts, p2, k2, p1, k2.

**5th row** As 3rd row.

Work 3 more rows in rib as set.

Cast off knitwise.

## TO MAKE UP

Join raglan and underarm seams. Join side and sleeve seams. Sew on buttons.

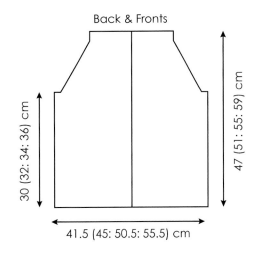

Back & Fronts

30 (32: 34: 36) cm

47 (51: 55: 59) cm

41.5 (45: 50.5: 55.5) cm

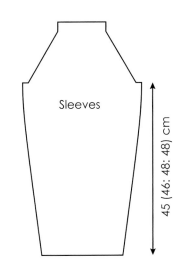

Sleeves

45 (46: 48: 48) cm

# A-line jacket

## MEASUREMENTS

To fit bust

| | | | |
|---|---|---|---|
| 81–86 | 92–97 | 102–107 | 112–117cm |

Finished measurements

Bust

| | | | |
|---|---|---|---|
| 92 | 102 | 112 | 122cm |

Length

| | | | |
|---|---|---|---|
| 56 | 58 | 61 | 63cm |

Sleeve length

| | | | |
|---|---|---|---|
| 44 | 45 | 46 | 48cm |

## MATERIALS

10(11:12:13) 50g balls of Debbie Bliss
cashmerino dk in Pearl Pink
Pair of 4mm knitting needles
One button

## TENSION

22 sts and 30 rows to 10cm square over st st
using 4mm needles.

## ABBREVIATIONS

beg = beginning; cont = continue;
cm = centimetre; dec = decrease;
foll = following; inc = increase; k = knit;
m1 = make one st by picking up and working
into back of loop lying between st just worked
and next st; p = purl; patt = pattern;
rem = remaining; rep = repeat; skpo = sl 1, k1,
pass slipped st over; sl = slip; st(s) = stitch(es);
st st = stocking stitch; tog = together.

## BACK

With 4mm needles, cast on 115(127:137:147)
sts.

**Moss st row** K1, [p1, k1] to end.

Rep the last row 7 times more.

Beg with a k row, work in st st.

Work 14(16:18:20) rows.

**Dec row** (right side) K5, skpo, k to last 7 sts,
k2tog, k5.

Work 11 rows in st st.

Rep the last 12 rows 4 times more then the dec
row once again. 103(115:125:135) sts.

Cont straight in st st until back measures
36(37:39:40)cm from cast on edge, ending with
a p row.

### Shape armholes

Cast off 6 sts at beg of next 2 rows.
91(103:113:123) sts.

**Next row** K2, skpo, k to last 4 sts, k2tog, k2.

P 1 row.

Rep the last 2 rows 5(6:7:8) times more, so
ending with a p row. 79(89:97:105) sts.

Cont straight in st st for a further 46(48:48:50)
rows, so ending with a p row.

### Shape shoulders

Cast off 18(22:25:28) sts at beg of next 2 rows.

Cast off rem 43(45:47:49) sts.

## LEFT FRONT

With 4mm needles, cast on 59(65:71:75) sts.

**Moss st row** K1, [p1, k1] to end.

Rep this row 7 times more.

**Next row** (right side) K to last 6 sts, [p1, k1]
3 times.

**Next row** [K1, p1] 3 times, p to end.

These 2 rows form st st with moss st front edge.

Work 12(14:16:18) rows.

**Dec row** (right side) K5, skpo, k to last 6 sts,
[p1, k1] 3 times.

Patt 11 rows.

Rep the last 12 rows 4 times more then the dec
row once again. 53(59:65:69) sts.

Cont straight in patt until front matches Back to
armhole, ending with a wrong side row.

### Shape armhole

**Next row** Cast off 6 sts, k to last 7 sts, p1,
[p1, k1] 3 times. 47(53:59:63) sts.

**Next row** [K1, p1] 3 times, k1, p to end.

**Next row** K2, skpo, k to last 8 sts, p2, [p1, k1]
3 times.

**Next row** [K1, p1] 3 times, k2, p to end.

**Next row** K2, skpo, k to last 9 sts, p3, [p1, k1]
3 times.

**Next row** [K1, p1] 3 times, k3, p to end.

Cont in this way to dec 1 st at armhole edge on
foll 4(5:6:7) right side rows and **at the same
time**, work 1 more st in reverse st st inside the
moss st edge on every foll right side row.

When all armhole decs have been worked, cont
straight, working 1 more st into reverse st st on
every right side row as before, until there are
19(21:23:23) sts in reverse st st, then work
straight until 16 rows less than Back to shoulder
have been worked, so ending with a wrong side
row. 41(46:51:54) sts.

**Next row** (right side) K17(20:23:26), [p1, k1]
12(13:14:14) times.

**Next row** [K1, p1] 12(13:14:14) times, k1, p to end.

Rep these 2 rows twice more, then the first of these 2 rows again.

**Shape neck**

**Next row** (wrong side) Cast off 18(19:21:21) sts in patt, moss st to last 16(19:22:25) sts, p to end.

Keeping armhole edge straight and 16(19:22:25) sts in st st at armhole edge, dec 1 st at neck edge on next 5 rows. 18(22:25:28) sts.

Patt 3 rows.

Cast off.

Place a marker 6 sts in from front edge on cast off neck edge.


RIGHT FRONT

With 4mm needles, cast on 59(65:71:75) sts.

**Moss st row** K1, [p1, k1] to end.

Rep this row 7 times more.

**Next row** (right side) [K1, p1] 3 times, k to end.

**Next row** P to last 6 sts, [p1, k1] 3 times.

These 2 rows form st st with moss st front edge. Work 12(14:16:18) rows.

**Dec row** (right side) [K1, p1] 3 times, k to last 7 sts, k2tog, k5.

Patt 11 rows.

Rep the last 12 rows 4 times more then the dec row once again. 53(59:65:69) sts.

Cont straight in patt until front matches Back to armhole, ending with the same wrong side row.

**Next row** [K1, p1] 3 times, p1, k to end.

**Shape armhole**

**Next row** (wrong side) Cast off 6 sts, p to last 7 sts, k1, [p1, k1] 3 times. 47(53:59:63) sts.

**Next row** [K1, p1] 3 times, p2, k to last 4 sts, k2tog, k2.

**Next row** P to last 8 sts, k2, [p1, k1] 3 times.

**Next row** [K1, p1] 3 times, p3, k to last 4 sts, k2tog, k2.

**Next row** P to last 9 sts, k3, [p1, k1] 3 times.

**Next row** [K1, p1] 3 times, p4, k to last 4 sts, k2tog, k2.

Cont in this way to dec 1 st at armhole edge on foll 3(4:5:6) right side rows and **at the same time**, work 1 more st in reverse st st inside the moss st edge on every foll right side row. When all armhole decs have been worked, cont straight, working 1 more st into reverse st st on every right side row as before until there are 19(21:23:23) sts in reverse st st, then work straight until 15 rows less than Back to right shoulder have been worked, so ending with a wrong side row. 41(46:51:54) sts.

**Next row** (right side) [K1, p1] 12(13:14:14) times, k to end.

**Next row** P16(19:22:25), k1, [p1, k1] 12(13:14:14) times.

Rep these 2 rows 3 times more.

**Shape neck**

**Next row** (right side) Cast off 18(19:21:21) sts in patt, moss st to last 16(19:22:25) sts, k to end.

Keeping armhole edge straight and 16(19:22:25) sts in st st at armhole edge, dec 1 st at neck edge on next 5 rows. 18(22:25:28) sts.

Patt 1 row.

Cast off.

Place a marker 6 sts in from front edge on cast off neck edge.

## SLEEVES

With 4mm needles, cast on 53(55:57:59) sts.

**Moss st row** K1, [p1, k1] to end.

Rep this row 13 times more.

Beg with a k row, work in st st and inc 1 st at each end of 11th and every foll 10th row, until there are 73(75:79:83) sts.

Cont straight until sleeve measures 44(45:46:48)cm from cast on edge, ending with a p row.

**Shape sleeve top**

Cast off 6 sts at beg of next 2 rows.

61(63:67:71) sts.

**Next row** (right side) K2, skpo, k to last 4 sts, k2tog, k2.

P1 row.

Rep the last 2 rows 5(6:7:8) times more.

49(49:51:53) sts.

**Next row** (right side) K2, skpo, k to last 4 sts, k2tog, k2.

Work 3 rows in st st.

Rep the last 4 rows 2(3:2:1) times.

43(41:45:49) sts.

**Next row** (right side) K2, skpo, k to last 4 sts, k2tog, k2.

P 1 row.

Rep the last 2 rows 5(4:6:8) times more. 31 sts.

Cast off 2 sts at beg of next 2 rows, then cast off 3 sts at beg of foll 6 rows.

Cast off rem 9 sts.

## COLLAR

With wrong side of back facing and 4mm needles, pick up and k47(49:51:53) sts across back neck edge.

**Next row** (wrong side of collar) Purl.

**Next row** K1, m1, k to last st, m1, k1.

**Next row** Purl.

**Next row** K1, m1, k13, m1, k to last 14 sts, m1, k13, m1, k1.

**Next row** Purl.

**Next row** K1, m1, k to last st, m1, k1.

**Next row** Purl.

**Next row** K1, m1, k15, m1, k to last 16 sts, m1, k15, m1, k1.

**Next row** Purl.

Cont in this way to inc 1 st at each end of every right side row and inc 2 more sts on every alt right side row, until there are 91(97:101:103) sts, ending with a right side row.

Place a marker at each end of last row.

**Next row** K1, [p1, k1] to end.

Rep the last row 6 times more.

Cast off in moss st.

## TO MAKE UP

Join shoulder seams. Join side edges of collar to front neck edge matching markers. Join sleeve seams. Match centre of sleeve top to shoulder, sew sleeves into armholes. Join side seams. Make button loop on right front opening edge, approx 5cm down from start of armhole shaping. Sew on button.

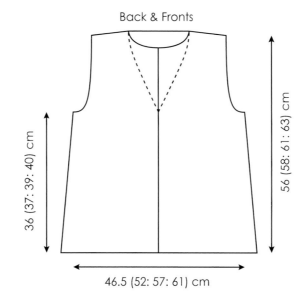

Back & Fronts

36 (37: 39: 40) cm

56 (58: 61: 63) cm

46.5 (52: 57: 61) cm

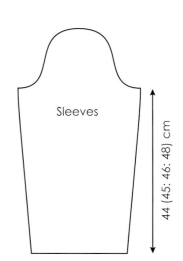

Sleeves

44 (45: 46: 48) cm

# COUNTRY

Earthy shades for a rural retreat – warm terracottas, chocolate brown and nutty taupes. Snuggle up into a selection of cosy styles, knitted in soft, natural yarns.

# cable and rib sweater

## MEASUREMENTS

To fit bust

76–81  86–92  97–102  107–112  117–122cm

Finished measurements

Bust

92    101    110    120    180cm

Length to centre front

49    53    57    61    65cm

Sleeve length

44    45    46    48    48cm

## MATERIALS

13(14:15:16:17) 50g balls of Debbie Bliss
cashmerino dk in Burnt Orange

Pair of 4mm knitting needles

Cable needle

## TENSION

29 sts and 34 rows to 10cm square over cable
patt using 4mm needles.

## ABBREVIATIONS

beg = beginning; C4B = slip next 2 sts onto
cable needle and hold at back of work, k2, then
k2 from cable needle; C4F = slip next 2 sts onto
cable needle and hold to front of work, k2, then
k2 from cable needle; cm = centimetre;
cont = continue; dec = decrease; foll =
following; inc = increase; k = knit; p = purl;
patt = pattern; psso = pass slipped st over;
rem = remaining; rep = repeat; skpo = sl 1, k1,
pass slipped st over; sl = slip; st(s) = stitch(es);
st st = stocking stitch; tog = together.

BACK and FRONT (both alike)

With 4mm needles, cast on
131(145:159:173:187) sts.

**1st row** (right side) P1, [k1, p1] 5 times, [k4,
p1, k1, p1] 16(18:20:22:24) times, [k1, p1]
4 times.

**2nd row** Purl.

**3rd row** P1, [k1, p1] 5 times, [C4B, p1, k1, p1]
8(9:10:11:12) times, [C4F, p1, k1, p1]
8(9:10:11:12) times, [k1, p1] 4 times.

**4th row** Purl.

These 4 rows form the patt and are repeated.

Cont straight in patt until back/front measures
31(33:35:37:39)cm from cast on edge, ending
with a wrong side row.

### Shape armholes and raglans

Cast off 6 sts at beg of next 2 rows.
119(133:147:161:175) sts.

**Next row** (right side) P1, k1, p2tog, patt to last
4 sts, p2tog, k1, p1.

**Next row** P2, k2tog, p to last 4 sts, k2tog, p2.

Rep the last 2 rows, decreasing 1 st at each end
of every row until 7(9:7:9:7) sts rem.

**1st, 3rd and 5th sizes only**

**Next row** (right side) P1, k1, p3tog, k1, p1. 5 sts.

**Next row** P1, p3tog, p1. 3 sts.

**Next row** Sl 1, k2tog, pass slipped st over and
fasten off.

**2nd and 4th sizes only**

**Next row** (right side) P1, k1, p2tog, k1, p2tog,
k1, p1. 7 sts.

**Next row** P2, p3tog, p2. 5 sts.

**Next row** P1, sl 1, k2tog, psso, p1. 3 sts.

**Next row** P3tog and fasten off.

SLEEVES

With 4mm needles, cast on 57(57:61:61:61) sts.

**1st row** (right side) P1, [k1, p1] 2(2:3:3:3) times, [k4, p1, k1, p1] 2 times, [k1, p1] 11 times, [k4, p1, k1, p1] 2 times, [k1, p1] 1(1:2:2:2) times.

**2nd row** Purl.

**3rd row** P1, [k1, p1] 2(2:3:3:3) times, [C4B, p1, k1, p1] 2 times, [k1, p1] 11 times, [C4F, p1, k1, p1] 2 times, [k1, p1] 1(1:2:2:2) times.

**4th row** Purl.

These 4 rows set the position of the central rib and the cables with rib to each side.

Cont in patt and inc as follows:

**Inc row** P1, m1, patt as set to last st, m1, p1.

P 1 row.

**Next row** P2, patt to last 2 sts working the cables, p2.

P 1 row.

**Next row** P2, patt to last 2 sts, p2.

P 1 row.

**Inc row** P1, m1, patt as set to last st working cables, m1, p1.

P 1 row.

**Next row** P1, k1, patt to last 2 sts, k1, p1.

P 1 row.

**Next row** P1, k1, patt to last 2 sts working cables, k1, p1.

P 1 row.

Rep the last 12 rows until there are 101(101:105:105:105) sts.

Cont straight in patt until sleeve measures 44(45:46:48:48)cm.

**Shape armhole and raglans**

Cast off 6 sts at each end of next 2 rows.

89(89:93:93:93) sts.

** Patt 12 rows as set.

**1st dec row** (right side) Patt 43(43:45:45:45), sl 1, k2tog, psso, patt to end.

Patt 5 rows.

**2nd dec row** (right side) Patt 42(42:44:44:44), p3tog, patt to end.

Patt 5 rows.

Cont in this way to dec 2 sts in centre of every 6th row, until 67(67:71:71:71) sts rem, ending with a 1st dec row.

Patt 5 rows.

**Next row** [P1, k1] 9(9:10:10:10) times, p1, p2tog, patt 25, p2tog, p1, [k1, p1] 9(9:10:10:10) times.

P 1 row.

**Next row** [P1, k1] 9(9:10:10:10) times, p2tog, patt 25, p2tog, [k1, p1] 9(9:10:10:10) times.

P 1 row.

**Next row** [P1, k1] 8(8:9:9:9) times, p1, p2tog, patt 25, p2tog, p1, [k1, p1] 8(8:9:9:9) times.

P1 row.

**Next row** [P1, k1] 8(8:9:9:9) times, p2tog, patt 25, p2tog, [k1, p1] 8(8:9:9:9) times.

P1 row. 59(59:63:63:63) sts.

Cont straight in patt as now set until sleeve measures 36(40:43:46:49)cm from **, ending with a right side row.

Cast off knitwise, working k2tog over centre 2 sts of each cable.

TO MAKE UP

Place markers, 10cm down from cast off edge of sleeves. Join front and back to sleeves along raglans with tip of centre front and centre back sewn to markers, then join sleeves above markers to form centre front and centre back collar.

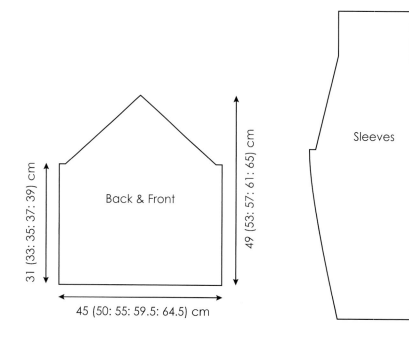

Back & Front

31 (33: 35: 37: 39) cm

49 (53: 57: 61: 65) cm

45 (50: 55: 59.5: 64.5) cm

Sleeves

44 (45: 46: 48: 48) cm

# cable and bobble scarf

**SIZE**

Approximately 15 x 220cm.

**MATERIALS**

Eight 50g balls of Debbie Bliss alpaca silk aran
in Mauve

Pair of 5.5mm knitting needles

Cable needle

**TENSION**

21 sts and 20 rows to 10cm square over patt
using 5.5mm needles.

**ABBREVIATIONS**

C6B = slip next 3 sts onto cable needle and
hold at back of work, k3, then k3 from cable
needle; cm = centimetres; k = knit; MB = [kfb]
twice, [turn, k4] 3 times, turn, [k2tog] twice,
pass 2nd st over 1st st; p = purl; patt = pattern;
st(s) = stitch(es); T3B = slip next st onto cable
needle and hold at back of work, k2, then p1
from cable needle; T3F = slip next 2 sts onto
cable needle and hold to front of work, p1, then
k2 from cable needle; T5B = slip next 2 sts onto
cable needle and hold at back of work, k3, then
p2 from cable needle; T5F = slip next 3 sts onto
cable needle and hold to front of work, p2, then
k3 from cable needle.

TO MAKE

With 5.5mm needles, cast on 32 sts.

**1st row** (right side) K2, p3, T3B, p5, C6B, p5,
T3F, p3, k2.

**2nd row** K5, p2, k6, p6, k6, p2, k5.

**3rd row** K2, p2, T3B, p4, T5B, T5F, p4, T3F,
p2, k2.

**4th row** K4, p2, k5, p3, k4, p3, k5, p2, k4.

**5th row** K2, p1, T3B, p3, T5B, p4, T5F, p3,
T3F, p1, k2.

**6th row** K3, p2, k1, MB, k2, p3, k8, p3, k2,
MB, k1, p2, k3.

**7th row** K2, p1, T3F, p3, k3, p8, k3, p3, T3B,
p1, k2.

**8th row** K4, p2, k3, p3, k4, pick up loop lying
between st just worked and next st and work
MB into it as before, slip bobble st back onto left
hand needle, k2tog, k3, p3, k3, p2, k4.

**9th row** K2, p2, T3F, p2, T5F, p4, T5B, p2,
T3B, p2, k2.

**10th row** K5, p2, [k4, p3] twice, k4, p2, k5.

**11th row** K2, p3, T3F, p3, T5F, T5B, p3, T3B,
p3, k2.

**12th row** K4, MB, k1, p2, k5, p6, k5, p2, k1,
MB, k4.

These 12 rows **form** the patt and are repeated.
Cont in patt until scarf measures approximately
220cm ending with a 2nd patt row.

Cast off in patt.

# moss stitch beret

**SIZE**

To fit an average-sized child's head.

**MATERIALS**

Two 50g balls Debbie Bliss alpaca silk aran in
Mauve (A) and oddments in Chocolate (B) for
pompom

Pair of each size 4.5mm and 5mm knitting
needles

**TENSION**

16 sts and 28 rows to 10cm square over moss
st using 5mm needles.

**ABBREVIATIONS**

alt = alternate; cm = centimetre;
dec = decrease; inc = increase; k = knit;
m1 = make one st by picking up and working
into back of loop lying between st just worked
and next st; p = purl; rem = remaining;
rep = repeat; st(s) = stitch(es); tog = together.

**TO MAKE**

With 4.5mm needles and A, cast on 80 sts.

**Rib row** [K1, p1] to end.

Rep this row 5 times more.

**Inc row** K2, * m1, k3, m1, k2; rep from * to last
3 sts, m1, k3. 111 sts.

Change to 5mm needles.

Work in moss st until beret measures 10cm
from cast on edge.

**Shape top**

**Dec row** K1, * work 3 tog, moss st 19; rep from
* to end. 101 sts.

Moss st 1 row.

**Dec row** K1, * work 3 tog, moss st 17; rep from
* to end. 91 sts.

Moss st 1 row.

**Dec row** K1, * work 3 tog, moss st 15; rep from
* to end. 81 sts.

Moss st 1 row.

Cont in this way to dec 10 sts on every alt row
until 11 sts rem.

Moss st 1 row.

Break yarn, thread through rem sts, pull up and
secure. Join seam. Make a pompom in B and
sew to top of beret.

# zipped jacket

## MEASUREMENTS

To fit chest

92–97    102–107  112–117cm

Finished measurements

Chest

101      111      121cm

Length to shoulder

60      63      66cm

Sleeve length

48      48      48cm

## MATERIALS

18(19:21) 50g balls of Debbie Bliss cotton dk
in Navy (A) and two balls in Green (B)
Pair of each size 3.25mm and 4mm knitting
needles
65(70:70)cm open-ended zip

## TENSION

20 sts and 28 rows to 10cm square over st st
using 4mm needles.

## ABBREVIATIONS

beg = beginning; cm = centimetre;
cont = continue; inc = increase; k = knit;
m1 = make one st by picking up and working
into back of loop lying between st just worked
and next st; p = purl; rem = remaining;
rep = repeat; skpo = sl 1, k1, pass slipped st
over; sl = slip; st(s) = stitch(es); st st = stocking
stitch; tog = together.

## BACK

With 3.25mm needles and B, cast on
102(110:122) sts.

**1st row** (right side) K2, * p2, k2; rep from
* to end.

**2nd row** P2, * k2, p2; rep from * to end.

Change to A.

**Next row** K to end.

**Next row** P2, * k2, p2; rep from * to end.

Work 4 more rows in rib, increasing 2 sts evenly
across last row on 2nd size only.
102(112:122) sts.

Change to 4mm needles.

Beg with a k row work in st st until back
measures 32(33:34)cm from cast on edge,
ending with a p row.

**Shape raglans**

Cast off 4(5:6) sts at beg of next 2 rows.
94(102:110) sts.

**1st row** K2, skpo, k to last 4 sts, k2tog, k2.

**2nd row** P to end.

**3rd row** K to end.

**4th row** P to end.

Rep the last 4 rows 5 times more. 82(90:98) sts.

**Next row** K2, skpo, k to last 4 sts, k2tog, k2.

**Next row** P to end.

Rep the last 2 rows until 30(32:34) sts rem
ending with a p row.

Leave these sts on a holder.

## LEFT FRONT

With 3.25mm needles and B, cast on 52(56:60)
sts.

**1st row** (right side) K2, * p2, k2; rep from * to
last 6 sts, p2, k4.

**2nd row** * K2, p2; rep from * to end.

Change to A.

**Next row** K to end.

**Next row** * K2, p2; rep from * to end.

Work 4 more rows in rib with 2-st garter st
border at front opening edge, increasing 0(1:2)
sts across last row. 52(57:62) sts.

Change to 4mm needles.

**Next row** (right side) K to end.

**Next row** K2, p to end.

Rep the last 2 rows until front measures
32(33:34)cm from cast on edge, ending with a
wrong side row.

**Shape raglan**

Cast off 4(5:6) sts at beg of next row.
48(52:56) sts.

Work one row.

**1st row** (right side) K2, skpo, k to end.

**2nd row** K2, p to end.

**3rd row** K to end.

**4th row** K2, p to end.

Rep the last 4 rows 5 times more. 42(46:50) sts.

**Next row** K2, skpo, k to end.

**Next row** K2, p to end.

Rep the last 2 rows until 16(17:18) sts rem
ending with a wrong side row.

Leave these sts on a holder.

## RIGHT FRONT

With 3.25mm needles and B, cast on 52(56:60)
sts.

**1st row** (right side) K4, * p2, k2; rep from
* to end.

**2nd row** * P2, k2; rep from * to end.

Change to A.

**Next row** K to end.

**Next row** * P2, k2; rep from * to end.

Work 4 more rows in rib with 2-st garter st border at front opening edge, increasing 0(1:2) sts across last row. 52(57:62) sts.

Change to 4mm needles.

**Next row** (right side) K to end.

**Next row** P to last 2 sts, k2.

Rep the last 2 rows until front measures 32(33:34)cm from cast on edge, ending with a right side row.

**Shape raglan**

Cast off 4(5:6) sts at beg of next row. 48(52:56) sts.

**1st row** (right side) K to last 4 sts, k2tog, k2.

**2nd row** P to last 2 sts, k2.

**3rd row** K to end.

**4th row** P to last 2 sts, k2.

Rep the last 4 rows 5 times more. 42(46:50) sts.

**Next row** K to last 4 sts, k2tog, k2.

**Next row** P to last 2 sts, k2.

Rep the last 2 rows until 16(17:18) sts rem ending with a wrong side row.

Leave these sts on a holder.

SLEEVES

With 3.25mm needles and B, cast on 46(50:54) sts.

**1st row** (right side) K2, * p2, k2; rep from * to end.

**2nd row** P2, * k2, p2; rep from * to end.

Change to A.

**Next row** K to end.

**Next row** P2, * k2, p2; rep from * to end.

Work 8 more rows in rib.

Change to 4mm needles.

Beg with a k row work in st st.

Work 4 rows.

**Inc row** K4, m1, k to last 4 sts, m1, k4.

Work 5 rows.

Rep the last 6 rows until there are 76(80:84) sts.

Cont straight until sleeve measures 48cm from cast on edge, ending with a p row.

**Shape raglans**

Cast off 4(5:6) sts at beg of next 2 rows. 68(70:72) sts.

**1st row** K2, skpo, k to last 4 sts, k2tog, k2.

**2nd row** P to end.

**3rd row** K to end.

**4th row** P to end.

Rep the last 4 rows 11(13:15) times more. 44(42:40) sts.

**Next row** K2, skpo, k to last 4 sts, k2tog, k2.

**Next row** P to end.

Rep the last 2 rows until 16 sts rem ending with a p row.

Leave these sts on a holder.

COLLAR

With right side facing, 4mm needles and A, k across 16(17:18) sts on right front, 16 sts on right sleeve, 30(32:34) sts at back neck, 16 sts on left sleeve and 16(17:18) sts of left front. 94(98:102) sts.

**1st row** (wrong side) K2, * p2, k2; rep from * to end.

**2nd row** K4, p2, * k2, p2; rep from * to last 4 sts, k4.

Rep the last 2 rows for 10cm, ending with a 1st row.

Change to 3.25mm needles and B.

**Next row** K to end.

Work a further 10cm rib.

Cast off in rib.

TO MAKE UP

Join raglan seams. Join side and sleeve seams. Sew zip behind garter st front edges, from cast on edge to halfway up collar. Fold collar in half onto wrong side and slip stitch in place, sewing row ends to back of zip tape to neaten.

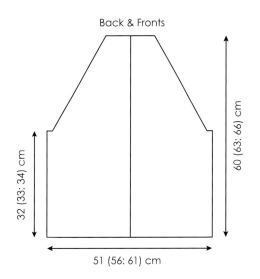

Back & Fronts

60 (63: 66) cm

32 (33: 34) cm

51 (56: 61) cm

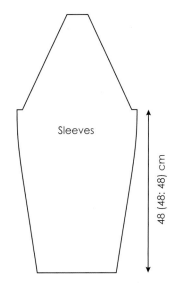

Sleeves

48 (48: 48) cm

# fair isle beanie

## SIZE

To fit an average-sized adult head.

## MATERIALS

One 50g ball of Debbie Bliss baby cashmerino in Stone (A) and a small amount in each of Indigo (B), Teal (C), Black (D), White (E), Red (F), Pink (G), and Yellow (H)
Pair of 3.25mm knitting needles

## TENSION

25 sts and 34 rows to 10cm square over st st using 3.25mm needles.

## ABBREVIATIONS

beg = beginning; cm = centimetre;
cont = continue; dec = decrease; k = knit;
p = purl; patt = pattern; rep = repeat;
st(s) = stitch(es); st st = stocking stitch;
tog = together.

## CHART NOTES

When working from chart, odd numbered (right side) rows are read from right to left and even numbered (wrong side) rows are read from left to right. Two edge sts shown at the right hand side of chart are worked at beg of right side rows and end of wrong side rows only, with the 8-st patt repeated across the row. Strand yarn not in use loosely across wrong side of work.

## TO MAKE

With 3.25mm needles and A, cast on 114 sts.
**Rib row** * K1, p1; rep from * to end.
Repeat the last row 7 times more.
Beg with a k row, work 2 repeats of the 20-row chart in st st.
Cont in st st in A only and shape top as follows:
**1st dec row** * K6, k2tog; rep from * to last 2 sts, k2. 100 sts.
P 1 row.
**2nd dec row** * K5, k2tog; rep from * to last 2 sts, k2. 86 sts.
P 1 row.
**3rd dec row** * K4, k2tog; rep from * to last 2 sts, k2. 72 sts.
P 1 row.
**4th dec row** * K3, k2tog; rep from * to last 2 sts, k2. 58 sts.
P 1 row.
**5th dec row** * K2, k2tog; rep from * to last 2 sts, k2. 44 sts.
P 1 row.

**6th dec row** * K1, k2tog; rep from * to last 2 sts, k2. 30 sts.
P 1 row.
**7th dec row** * K2tog; rep from * to last 2 sts, k2. 16 sts.
**Next row** * P2tog; rep from * to end.
Break off yarn thread through rem 8 sts, pull up and secure.
Join seam, taking one st from each side into seam, carefully matching the patt.

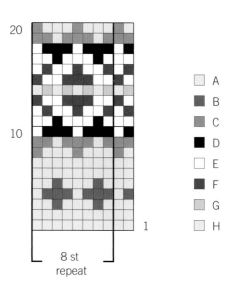

A
B
C
D
E
F
G
H

8 st repeat

# moss stitch jacket & mitts

## MEASUREMENTS

To fit ages

| 2 | 3 | 4 | 5 years |
|---|---|---|---|

Finished measurements

Chest

| 75 | 79 | 85 | 89cm |
|---|---|---|---|

Length to shoulder

| 40 | 42 | 46 | 50cm |
|---|---|---|---|

Sleeve length

| 22 | 24 | 27 | 30cm |
|---|---|---|---|

## MATERIALS

**Jacket** 10(11:12:13) 50g balls of Debbie Bliss cotton dk in Chocolate (A) and 1(2:2:2) balls in Lime (B)

Pair of each size 3.75mm and 4mm knitting needles

35(35:40:45)cm open-ended zip

**Mitts** Two 50g balls of Debbie Bliss cotton dk in Lime (B) and oddments in Chocolate (A)

Pair each 3.75mm and 4mm knitting needles

## TENSION

20 sts and 32 rows to 10cm square over moss st using 4mm needles.

## ABBREVIATIONS

beg = beginning; cm = centimetre; cont = continue; dec = decrease; foll = following; inc = increase; k = knit; m1 = make one st by picking up and working into back of loop lying between st just worked and next st; p = purl; patt = pattern; rem = remaining; rep = repeat; skpo = sl 1, k1, pass slipped st over; sl = slip; st(s) = stitch(es); st st = stocking stitch; tog = together.

## BACK

With 3.75mm needles and A, cast on 77(81:87:91) sts.

K 3 rows.

Change to 4mm needles.

**Moss st row** (right side) K1, * p1, k1; rep from * to end.

This row forms moss st.

Cont in moss st until back measures 26(27:30:33)cm from cast on edge, ending with a wrong side row.

### Shape armholes

Cast off 5(5:6:6) sts at beg of next 2 rows. 67(71:75:79) sts.

Cont straight until back measures 40(42:46:50)cm from cast on edge, ending with a wrong side row.

### Shape shoulders

Cast off 10(11:11:12) sts at beg of next 2 rows and 11(11:12:12) sts at beg of foll 2 rows.

Cast off rem 25(27:29:31) sts.

## POCKET LININGS (make 2)

With 3.75mm needles and B, cast on 17(17:19:19) sts.

Work 7(8:8:9)cm garter st (k every row).

Leave sts on a holder.

## LEFT FRONT

With 3.75mm needles and A, cast on 38(40:44:46) sts.

K 3 rows.

Change to 4mm needles.

**Next row** (right side) * P1, k1; rep from * to last 2 sts, k2.

**Next row** K3, * p1, k1; rep from * to last st, p1.

These 2 rows form the moss st with garter st edging.

Cont in patt until front measures 8(9:9:10)cm from cast on edge, ending with a wrong side row.

### Place pocket

**Next row** (right side) Moss st 10(11:12:13) sts, cast off next 17(17:19:19), patt to end.

**Next row** Patt 11(12:13:14) sts, p across sts of one pocket lining, moss st 10(11:12:13).

Cont in patt across all sts until front measures 26(27:30:33)cm from cast on edge, ending with a wrong side row.

### Shape armhole

Cast off 5(5:6:6) sts at beg of next row. 33(35:38:40) sts.

Cont in patt until front measures 36(37:41:45)cm from cast on edge, ending with a wrong side row.

### Shape neck

**Next row** Patt to last 10(11:13:14), turn and leave these sts on a holder, cont on rem 23(24:25:26) sts.

Dec one st at neck edge on next 2 rows. 21(22:23:24) sts.

Work straight until front matches Back to shoulder, ending at side edge.

### Shape shoulder

Cast off 10(11:11:12) sts at beg of next row.

Work 1 row.

Cast off rem 11(11:12:12) sts.

## RIGHT FRONT

With 3.75mm needles and A, cast on 38(40:44:46) sts.

K 3 rows.

Change to 4mm needles.

**Next row** (right side) K3, * p1, k1; rep from * to last st, p1.

**Next row** * P1, k1; rep from * to last 4 sts, p1, k3.

These 2 rows form the moss st with garter st edging.

Cont in patt until front measures 8(9:9:10)cm from cast on edge, ending with a wrong side row.

**Place pocket**

**Next row** (right side) Patt 11(12:13:14) sts, cast off next 17(17:19:19), patt to end.

**Next row** Moss st 10(11:12:13)sts, p across sts of rem pocket lining, patt to end.

Cont in patt across all sts until front measures 26(27:30:33)cm from cast on edge, ending with a right side row.

**Shape armhole**

Cast off 5(5:6:6) sts at beg of next row.

33(35:38:40) sts.

Cont in patt until front measures 36(137:41:45)cm from cast on edge, ending with a wrong side row.

**Shape neck**

**Next row** Patt 10(11:13:14) sts, leave these sts on a holder, patt to end.

Dec one st at neck edge on next 2 rows. 21(22:23:24) sts.

Work straight until front matches Back to shoulder, ending at side edge.

**Shape shoulder**

Cast off 10(11:11:12) sts at beg of next row.

Work 1 row.

Cast off rem 11(11:12:12) sts.

## COLLAR

Join shoulder seams.

With right side facing, 3.75mm needles and A, slip 10(11:13:14) sts from right front onto a needle, pick up and k10(12:12:14) sts up right front neck, 31(33:35:37) sts across back neck, 10(12:12:14) sts down left front neck, k10(11:13:14) sts from holder.

71(79:85:93) sts.

**Next row** K3, * p1, k1; rep from * to last 4 sts, p1, k3.

This row sets the moss st with garter st edge.

**Next 2 rows** Patt to last 20 sts, turn.

**Next 2 rows** Patt to last 16 sts, turn.

**Next 2 rows** Patt to last 12 sts, turn.

**Next 2 rows** Patt to last 8 sts, turn.

**Next row** Patt to end.

Cont in patt work a further 6(6:7:7)cm.

K 3 rows.

Cast off.

## SLEEVES

With 4mm needles and A, cast on 35(37:39:41) sts.

K 3 rows.

**Next row** (right side of cuff, wrong side of sleeve) K1, * p1, k1; rep from * to end.

This row forms moss st.

Work a further 13(13:15:15) rows.

Change to 3.75mm needles and B.

K 23(23:27:27) rows.

Change to 4mm needles and A.

K 1 row.

Cont in moss st.

Inc and work into moss st one st at each end of 4th(4th:6th:6th) row and every foll 4th row until there are 57(61:67:71) sts.

Cont straight until sleeve measures 22(24:27:30)cm from beg of garter st, ending with a wrong side row.

Mark each end of last row with a coloured thread.

Work a further 8(8:10:10) rows.

Cast off.

## TO MAKE UP

Sew sleeves into armholes, with row-ends above markers sewn to cast off sts at underarm. Join side and sleeve seams. Sew down pocket linings. Sew zip behind garter st edges. Fold moss st cuffs onto right side.

## MITTS

*RIGHT MITT*

With 3.75mm needles and A, cast on 27(31:33:35) sts.

**Moss st row** K1, * p1, k1; rep from * to end.

Rep the last row once more.

Change to B.

K 18 rows.

Change to 4mm needles.

K 4 rows. **

**Thumb shaping**

**Next row** K14(16:17:18), m1, k1(1:2:2), m1, k12(14:14:15).

K 3 rows.

**Next row** K14(16:17:18), m1, k3(3:4:4), m1, k12(14:14:15).

K 3 rows.

**Next row** K14(16:17:18), m1, k5(5:6:6), m1, k12(14:14:15).

K 3 rows.

**Next row** K14(16:17:18), m1, k7(7:8:8), m1, k12(14:14:15). 35(39:41:43) sts.

K 3 rows.

**3rd and 4th sizes only**

**Next row** K-(-:17:18), m1, k-(-:10:10), m1, k-(-:14:15).

K 3 rows. 35(39:43:45) sts.

**All sizes**

**Divide for thumb**

**Next row** K23(25:29:30), turn, cast on 2 sts.

**Next row** K11(11:14:14) sts, turn.

K8(10:12:14) rows.

**Next row** K1(1:0:0), * skpo; rep from * to end.

**Next row** K to end.

Break yarn thread through rem sts, draw up tightly and join seam.

With right side facing, pick up and k3 sts from base of thumb, k to end. 29(33:34:36) sts. ***

K 7(9:11:13) rows.

**Shape top**

**Next row** K1(1:2:2), [skpo, k8(10:10:11), k2tog, k2] twice.

K 1 row.

**Next row** K1(1:2:2), [skpo, k6(8:8:9), k2tog, k2] twice.

K 1 row.

**Next row** K1(1:2:2), [skpo, k4(6:6:7), k2tog, k2] twice.

K 1 row.

Cast off rem 17(21:22:24) sts.

*LEFT MITT*

Work as Right Mitt to **.

**Thumb shaping**

**Next row** K12(14:14:15), m1, k1(1:2:2), m1, k14(16:17:18).

K 3 rows.

**Next row** K12(14:14:15), m1, k3(3:4:4), m1,

k14(16:17:18).

K 3 rows.

**Next row** K12(14:14:15), m1, k5(5:6:6), m1, k14(16:17:18).

K 3 rows.

**Next row** K12(14:14:15), m1, k7(7:8:8), m1, k14(16:17:18). 35(39:41:43) sts.

K 3 rows.

**3rd and 4th sizes only**

**Next row** K-(-:14:15), m1, k-(-:10:10), m1, k-(-:17:18).

K 3 rows. 35(39:43:45) sts.

**All sizes**

**Divide for thumb**

**Next row** K21(23:26:27), turn, cast on 2 sts.

**Next row** K11(11:14:14) sts, turn.

K 8(10:12:14) rows.

**Next row** K1(1:0:0), * skpo; rep from * to end.

**Next row** K to end.

Break yarn thread through rem sts, draw up tightly and join seam.

With right side facing, pick up and k3 sts from base of thumb, k to end. 29(33:34:36) sts.

Work as given for Right Mitt from *** to end.

CORD (optional)

Make a chain stitch cord in A. Attach ends to mitts and sew centre of cord inside back neck of jacket.

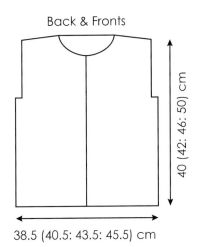

Back & Fronts

40 (42: 46: 50) cm

38.5 (40.5: 43.5: 45.5) cm

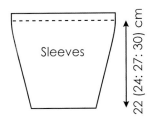

Sleeves

22 (24: 27: 30) cm

# cabled coat

## MEASUREMENTS

To fit bust

| 82–87 | 92–97 | 102–107cm |
|---|---|---|

Finished measurements

Bust

| 104 | 115 | 126cm |
|---|---|---|

Length to shoulder

| 92 | 94 | 96cm |
|---|---|---|

Sleeve length

| 43 | 44 | 45cm |
|---|---|---|

## MATERIALS

27(29:30) 50g balls of Debbie Bliss cashmerino aran in Stone

Pair of each size 3.75mm, 4mm and 5mm knitting needles

One each 4mm and 5mm circular needle

Cable needle

7 buttons

## TENSION

18 sts and 24 rows to 10cm square over st st using 5mm needles.

## ABBREVIATIONS

alt = alternate; beg = beginning; C4B = slip next 2 sts on cable needle and hold at back of work, k2, then k2 from cable needle; C4F = slip next 2 sts on cable needle and hold at front of work, k2, then k2 from cable needle; cm = centimetres; cont = continue; dec = decrease; foll = following; inc = increase; k = knit; m1 = make one st by picking up and working into back of loop lying between st just worked and next st; p = purl; patt = pattern; rem = remaining; rep = repeat; skpo = sl 1, k1, pass slipped st over; st(s) = stitch(es); st st = stocking stitch; T3B = slip next st on cable needle and hold at back of work, k2, then p1 from cable needle; T3F = slip next 2 sts on cable needle and hold at front of work, p1, then k2 from cable needle; tbl = through back loop; tog = together; y2rn = yarn round needle twice.

## PANEL A (worked over 12 sts)

**1st row** (right side) K2, p2, k4, p2, k2.

**2nd row** P2, k2, p4, k2, p2.

**3rd row** K2, p2, C4F, p2, k2.

**4th row** As 2nd row.

These 4 rows form the pattern and are repeated throughout.

## PANEL B (worked over 15(17:19) sts)

**1st row** (right side) P3(4:5), T3F, T3B, T3F, p3(4:5).

**2nd row** K3(4:5), p2, k2, p4, k4(5:6).

**3rd row** P4(5:6), C4B, p2, k2, p3(4:5).

**4th row** K3(4:5), p2, k2, p4, k4(5:6).

**5th row** P3(4:5), T3B, T3F, T3B, p3(4:5).

**6th row** K4(5:6), p4, k2, p2, k3(4:5).

**7th row** P3(4:5), k2, p2, C4F, p4(5:6).

**8th row** K4(5:6), p4, k2, p2, k3(4:5).

These 8 rows form the pattern and are repeated throughout.

## PANEL C (worked over 32(34:36) sts)

**1st row** (right side) P5(6:7), T3F, p2, [T3F, T3B] twice, p2, T3B, p5(6:7).

**2nd row and every foll alt row** K all the k sts and p the p sts.

**3rd row** P6(7:8), T3F, [p2, C4B] twice, p2, T3B, p6(7:8).

**5th row** P7(8:9), [T3F, T3B] 3 times, p7(8:9).

**7th row** P8(9:10), [C4F, p2] twice, C4F, p8(9:10).

**9th row** P7(8:9), [T3B, T3F] 3 times, p7(8:9).

**11th row** P6(7:8), T3B, [p2, C4B] twice, p2, T3F, p6(7:8).

**13th row** P5(6:7), T3B, p2, [T3B, T3F] twice, p2, T3F, p5(6:7).

**15th row** P4(5:6), [T3B, p2] twice, C4F, [p2, T3F] twice, p4(5:6).

**17th row** P3(4:5), [T3B, p2] twice, T3B, T3F, [p2, T3F] twice, p3(4:5).

**19th row** P3(4:5), [k2, p3] twice, k2, p2, k2, [p3, k2] twice, p3(4:5).

**21st row** P3(4:5), [T3F, p2] twice, T3F, T3B, [p2, T3B] twice, p3(4:5).

**23rd row** P4(5:6), [T3F, p2] twice, C4F, [p2, T3B] twice, p4(5:6).

**24th row** As 2nd row.

These 24 rows form the pattern and are repeated throughout.

BACK

With 5mm needles, cast on 157(167:177) sts.

**1st row** Work across 1st row of panels B, A, C, A, B, A, C, A, B.

**2nd row** Work across 2nd row of panels B, A, C, A, B, A, C, A, B.

These 2 rows set the position of the patt panels. Cont in patt working correct patt panel rows, until work measures 72(73:74)cm from cast on edge, ending with a wrong side row.

**Shape armholes**

Cast off 14(16:18) sts at beg of next 2 rows. 129(135:141) sts.

Cont straight until back measures 92(94:96)cm from cast on edge, ending with a wrong side row.

**Shape shoulders**

Cast off 15(16:17) sts at beg of next 4 rows and 15 sts at beg of foll 2 rows.

Cast off rem 39(41:43) sts.

LEFT FRONT

With 5mm needles cast on 72(76:80) sts.

**1st row** Work across 1st row of Panels B, A, C, A, p1.

**2nd row** K1, work across 2nd row of Panels A, C, A, B.

These 2 rows **set** the position of the patt panels. Cont in patt working correct patt panel rows, until work measures 72(73:74)cm from cast on edge, ending with a wrong side row.

**Shape armhole**

Cast off 14(16:18) sts at beg of next row. 58(60:62) sts.

Work 1(3:5) rows.

**Shape neck**

Dec one st at neck edge on next row and 4 foll alt rows then on 8 foll 4th rows. 45(47:49) sts. Cont straight until front measures same as Back to shoulder, ending at armhole edge.

**Shape shoulder**

Cast off 15(16:17) sts at beg of next and foll alt row.

Work 1 row.

Cast off rem 15 sts.

RIGHT FRONT

With 5mm needles cast on 72(76:80) sts.

**1st row** P1, work across 1st row of Panels A, C, A, B.

**2nd row** Work across 2nd row of Panels B A, C, A, k1.

These 2 rows **set** the position of the patt panels. Cont in patt working correct patt panel rows, until work measures 72(73:74)cm from cast on edge, ending with a right side row.

**Shape armhole**

Cast off 14(16:18) sts at beg of next row.

58(60:62) sts.

Work 0(2:4) rows.

**Shape neck**

Dec one st at neck edge on next row and 4 foll alt rows then on 8 foll 4th rows. 45(47:49) sts. Cont straight until front measures same as Back to shoulder, ending at armhole edge.

**Shape shoulder**

Cast off 15(16:17) sts at beg of next and foll alt row.

Work 1 row.

Cast off rem 15 sts.

SLEEVES

With 3.75mm needles cast on 66(70:74) sts.

**1st row** P3(4:5), k2, p2, k2, p3(4:5), k2, [p2, k2] 10 times, p3(4:5), k2, p2, k2, p3(4:5).

**2nd row** K3(4:5), p2, k2, p2, k3(4:5), p2, k2, m1, p2, m1, rib 30, m1, p2, m1, k2, p2, k3(4:5), p2, k2, p2, k3(4:5). 70(74:78) sts.

**3rd row** P3(4:5), k2, p2, k2, p3(4:5), work across 3rd row of Panel A, rib 22, work across 3rd row of Panel A, p3(4:5), k2, p2, k2, p3(4:5).

**4th row** K3(4:5), p2, k2, p2, k3(4:5), work across 4th row of Panel A, rib 22, work across 4th row of Panel A, k3(4:5), p2, k2, p2, k3(4:5).

Work a further 7 rows as set.

**1st size only**

**12th row** (wrong side) K1, m1, k2, m1, p2, m1, rib 7, work across 4th row of Panel A, rib 2, [m1, rib 2] 10 times, work across 4th row of Panel A, m1, rib 3, m1, p2, m1, k2, p2, k3. 86 sts.

**2nd size only**

**12th row** (wrong side) [K2, m1] twice, p2, m1, rib 8, work across 4th row of Panel A, rib 1, m1, rib 1, [m1, rib 2] 9 times, [m1, rib 1] twice,

work across 4th row of Panel A, m1, rib 4, m1, p2, m1, k2, p2, k4. 92 sts.

### 3rd size only

**12th row** (wrong side) K3, m1, k2, m1, p2, m1, rib 9, work across 4th row of Panel A, m1, rib 1, m1, rib 1, [m1, rib 2] 9 times, [m1, rib 1] twice, m1, work across 4th row of Panel A, m1, rib 5, m1, p2, m1, k2, p2, k5. 98 sts.

### All sizes

Change to 5mm needles.

**1st row** Work across 1st row of Panels B, A, C, A, B.

**2nd row** Work across 2nd row of Panels B, A, C, A, B.

These 2 rows **set** the position of the patt panels. Keeping patt correct, inc one st at each end of the next row, 3 foll 6th rows and then every foll 8th row until there are 110(116:122) sts, working all inc sts into panel A.

Cont straight until sleeve measures 43(44:45)cm from cast on edge, ending with a wrong side row.

Mark each end of last row with a coloured thread.

Work a further 10 rows.

Cast off.

### COLLAR

Join shoulder seams.

With right side facing, 4mm circular needle and beginning at neck shaping, pick up and k 56 sts up right side of front neck, 40 sts from back neck and 56 sts down left side of front neck to beginning of neck shaping. 152 sts.

K 1 row.

**Inc row** P6, * m1, p3; rep from * to last 5 sts, m1, p5. 200 sts.

**1st row** (right side of collar) P1, work across 1st

row of 1st size of Panels A, C, A, B, A, C, A, B, A, C, A, p1.

**2nd row** K1, work across 2nd row of 1st size of Panels A, C, A, B, A, C, A, B, A, C, A, k1.

These 2 rows **set** the position of the patt panels.

Patt a further 6 rows working correct patt panel rows.

Change to 5mm circular needle.

Cont in patt until collar measures 20cm, ending with 12th row of Patt C.

**Dec row** P1, k2, * p2, k2tog, skpo, [p2, k2] 3 times, p1, p2tog, k2tog, skpo, p2, k2tog, skpo, p2tog, p1, [k2, p2] 3 times, k2tog, skpo, p2, k2, ** [p2tog] twice, k2tog, skpo, p2, k2, p1, p2 tog, k2; rep from * once, then from * to **, p1. 160 sts.

Change to 4mm circular needle.

**1st rib row** K1, * p2, k2; rep from * to last 3 sts, p2, k1.

**2nd rib row** P1, * k2, p2; rep from * to last 3 sts, k2, p1.

Rep the last 2 rows 4 times more.

Cast off in rib.

## BUTTON BAND

With right side of left collar facing and 4mm circular needle, pick up and k58 sts along row ends of collar from start of collar to collar cast off edge.

Break off yarn and leave sts on needle.

With right side of jacket facing and other end of the 4mm circular needle, pick up and k138(142:146) sts along left front edge. 196(200:204) sts.

Cont to work backwards and forwards with 4mm circular needle.

**Rib row** * K2, p2; rep from * to end.

Rep the last row 9 times more.

Cast off in rib.

## BUTTONHOLE BAND

With right side of right collar facing and 4mm needles, pick up and k58 sts along row ends of collar from cast off edge to start of collar.

Break off yarn and leave sts on needle.

With right side of jacket facing and 4mm circular needle, pick up and k138(142:146) sts along right front edge from lower cast on edge to start of collar.

Break off yarn, slip sts from needle onto circular needle. 196(200:204) sts.

Rejoin yarn to other end of circular needle at collar edge.

Cont to work backwards and forwards with 4mm circular needle.

**Rib row** * K2, p2; rep from * to end.

Rep the last row 3 times more.

**Buttonhole row** Rib 64(68:72), k2tog, y2rn, p2tog tbl, [rib 16, k2tog, y2rn, p2tog tbl] 6 times, rib to end.

Work a further 5 rows in rib.

Cast off in rib.

## TO MAKE UP

Sew sleeves into armholes with row ends above markers sewn to sts cast off at underarm. Join side and sleeve seams. Sew on buttons.

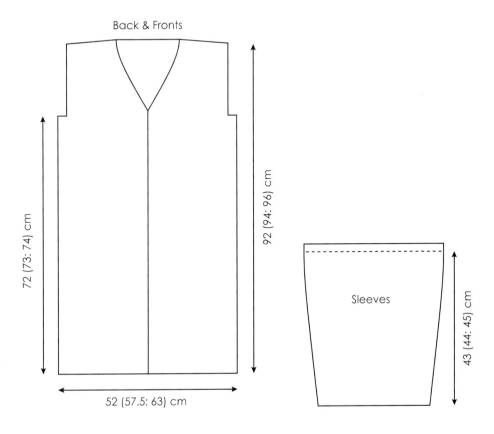

Back & Fronts

72 (73: 74) cm

92 (94: 96) cm

52 (57.5: 63) cm

Sleeves

43 (44: 45) cm

# aran bag

## SIZE

Approx 34 x 24cm.

## MATERIALS

Six 50g balls of Debbie Bliss alpaca silk aran in Terracotta and oddments in each of Mauve and Chocolate for pompoms

Pair of 4.5mm knitting needles

Cable needle

50cm of 90-cm wide lining fabric and same of firm/heavyweight iron-on interfacing.

Sewing thread and needle

Four 11mm eyelets

## TENSION

18 sts and 24 rows to 10cm square over st st using 4.5 needles.

## ABBREVIATIONS

C2(8)B = sl next 1(4) sts onto cable needle and hold at back of work, k1(4), then k1(4) from cable needle; C2(8)F = sl next 1(4) sts onto cable needle and hold to front of work, k1(4), then k1(4) from cable needle; Cr2L = sl next st onto cable needle and hold to front (right side) of work, p1, then k1 from cable needle; Cr2R = sl next st onto cable needle and hold at back (wrong side) of work, k1, then p1 from cable needle; cm = centimetre; cont = continue; k = knit; MB = [k1, yf, k1, yf, k1] into next st, turn, k5, turn, p5, turn, k5, turn, sl 2, p3tog, pass 2 sl sts over; p = purl; patt = pattern; st(s) = stitch(es); st st = stocking stitch; tbl = through back loop; tog = together; Tw2 = k 2nd st on left

needle, k 1st st on left needle and slip both sts off needle together; y2rn = yarn round needle twice; yf = yarn forward.

## PATT PANEL A (worked over 16 sts)

**1st row** (right side) P7, k2, p7.
**2nd row** K7, p2, k7.
**3rd row** P6, C2B, C2F, p6.
**4th row** K5, Cr2L, p2, Cr2R, k5.
**5th row** P4, Cr2R, C2B, C2F, Cr2L, p4.
**6th row** K3, Cr2L, k1, p4, k1, Cr2R, k3.
**7th row** P2, Cr2R, p1, Cr2R, k2, Cr2L, p1, Cr2L, p2.
**8th row** K1, Cr2L, k2, p1, k1, p2, k1, p1, k2, Cr2R, k1.
**9th row** Cr2R, p2, Cr2R, p1, k2, p1, Cr2L, p2, Cr2L.
**10th row** P1, k3, p1, k2, p2, k2, p1, k3, p1.
**11th row** MB, p2, Cr2R, p2, k2, p2, Cr2L, p2, MB.
**12th row** K3, p1, k3, p2, k3, p1, k3.
**13th row** P3, MB, p3, k2, p3, MB, p3.
**14th row** As 2nd row.
**15th and 16th rows** As 1st and 2nd rows.
These 16 rows form Patt Panel A.

## PATT PANEL B (worked over 16 sts)

**1st, 3rd, 7th and 9th rows** (right side) K.
**2nd, 4th, 6th, 8th and 10th** rows P.
**5th row** C8F, k3, MB, k4.
**11th row** K4, MB, k3, C8B.
**12th row** P.
These 12 rows form Patt Panel B.

## BACK and FRONT (both alike)

With 4.5mm needles, cast on 66 sts.

**1st row** (right side) P3, work across 16 sts of 1st row of Patt Panel B, p2, Tw2, p2, work across 16 sts of 1st row of Patt Panel A, p2, Tw2, p2, work across 16 sts of 1st row of Patt Panel B, p3.

**2nd row** K3, work across 16 sts of 2nd row of Patt Panel B, k2, p2, k2, work across 16 sts of 2nd row of Patt Panel A, k2, p2, k2, work across 16 sts of 2nd row of Patt Panel B, k3.

These 2 rows **set** the position of the patt panels and **form** twist sts on reverse st st between.

Cont in patt, working correct patt panel rows until 10th rows of 4th repeat of Patt Panel A and 5th repeat of Patt Panel B have been worked.

**Next row** (right side) P3, work 11th row of Patt Panel B, p1, p2tog, y2rn, p2tog, p1, work 11th row of Patt Panel A, p1, p2tog, y2rn, p2tog, p1, work 11th row of Patt Panel B, p3.

**Next row** K3, work 12th row of Patt Panel B, k2, p1, p1 tbl, k2, work 12th row of Patt Panel A, k2, p1, p1 tbl, k2, work 12th row of Patt Panel B, k3.

Patt 2 rows.

Cast off purlwise.

## GUSSET (make one)

With 4.5mm needles, cast on 21 sts.

**Moss st row** K1, [p1, k1] to end.

This row forms moss st and is repeated.

Cont until gusset measures 78cm.

Cast off.

### SIDE TIES (make 4)

Use four 48cm lengths of yarn, twisted and doubled to make a cord.

### HANDLES (make 2)

Use twelve 2m lengths of yarn, twisted and doubled to make a cord.

### TO MAKE UP

Place markers on each side of gusset, 24cm down from cast off and cast on edges. Stitch cast on edge of bag front to gusset, between markers, then stitch sides of front to remaining gusset edges, stitching side ties into the seams, 4cm down from top edge. Stitch bag back to gusset in the same way.

### LINING

Lay the interfacing on the lining fabric and iron in place. Cut two pieces of lining fabric, 33 x 28cm for back and front and one fabric piece 14 x 84cm for gusset. Taking 1.5cm seams, stitch gusset to back and front. Place lining inside bag, turning top edge of lining onto wrong side. On the lining, mark the position for the eyelets, using the knitted eyelets as a guide. Remove the lining then following the manufacturer's directions, insert the eyelets. Replace the lining in the bag and stitch in place around the top edge, then catch-stitch around the base, up the edges of the gusset and around the eyelets. Thread each handle cord through the eyelets and knot on the inside of the bag. Make two pompoms in each contrasting colour and attach one to the end of each side tie.

# lace socks

## SIZE

One size to fit average-sized adult feet.

## MATERIALS

Five 25g hanks of Debbie Bliss Pure Cashmere in Pale Pink

Set of four 5mm double-pointed knitting needles

## TENSION

18 sts and 25 rows to 10cm square over st st using 5mm needles.

## ABBREVIATIONS

beg = beginning; cm = centimetre; cont = continue; dec = decrease; k = knit; p = purl; patt = pattern; rem = remaining; rep = repeat; sl 1 pwise = slip 1 st purlwise; ssk = slip next 2 sts knitwise, place tip of left hand needle into fronts of slipped sts and k2tog; st(s) = stitch(es); st st = stocking stitch; tog = together; yo = yarn over needle.

## TO MAKE

With 5mm double-pointed needles, cast on 45 sts and arrange them over the needles as follows: 17 sts on 1st needle, 18 sts on 2nd needle and 10 sts on 3rd needle.

Join the round, taking care not to twist the sts between needles.

**Foundation round** K.

**1st round** * yo, k2, ssk, k2tog, k2, yo, k1; rep from * to end of round.

**NOTE** you will end the sts of both the 1st and 2nd needles with a yo, take care not to drop these.

**2nd round** K.

**3rd round** K1, * yo, k2, ssk, k2tog, k2, yo, k1; rep from * to last 8 sts, yo, k2, ssk, k2tog, k2, yo.

**NOTE** you will end the sts of both 1st and 2nd needles as k1, this being half the k2 after the k2tog in the pattern.

**4th round** Re-arrange sts as follows: k 16 sts on the 1st needle and one more onto this needle from the 2nd needle so returning to 17 sts, k rem 17 sts on 2nd needle and one more from 3rd needle so returning to 18 sts, k rem 10 sts on 3rd needle.

Rep the last 4 rounds 7 times more, then the first 3 rounds again, take care not to lose the final yo.

**Dec round** K2, k2tog, k4, place a marker, k22, place a marker, k4, [k2tog] 3 times, k2, k2tog, k1. 40 sts.

Cut yarn.

Re-arrange sts as follows: place the 22 sts between markers onto a single needle to hold for foot, arrange rem 18 sts as 9 sts on each of 2 needles.

Rejoin yarn at beg of these 18 sts and work heel as follows:

**Next row** (right side) K17, turn.

**Next row** Sl 1 pwise, p15, turn.

**Next row** Sl 1 pwise, k14, turn.

**Next row** Sl 1 pwise, p13, turn.

Cont in this way, working 1 less st on each row until the row "sl 1 pwise, p9, turn" has been worked.

**Next row** Sl 1 pwise, k10, turn.

**Next row** Sl 1 pwise, p11, turn.

**Next row** Sl 1 pwise, k12, turn.

Cont in this way working one more st on each row until the row "sl 1 pwise, p17, turn" has been worked.

**Work foot**

**Next round** K9 sts on 1st needle, k9 on 2nd needle, work across 22 sts on 3rd needle as follows: k1, [yo, k2, ssk, k2tog, k2, yo, k1] twice, k3.

**Next round** K.

**Next round** K18 (on first 2 needles), k2, [yo, k2, ssk, k2tog, k2, yo, k1] twice, k2.

**Next round** K.

Rep the last 4 rounds 7 times more.

**Shape toe**

**Next round** K2tog, k14, ssk, k2, k2tog, k14, ssk, k2. 36 sts.

**Next round** K.

**Next round** K2tog, k12, ssk, k2, k2tog, k12, ssk, k2. 32 sts.

**Next round** K.

**Next round** K2tog, k10, ssk, k2, k2tog, k10, ssk, k2. 28 sts.

**Next round** K.

**Next round** K2tog, k8, ssk, k2, k2tog, k8, ssk, k2. 24 sts.

**Next round** K.

**Next round** K2tog, k6, ssk, k2, k2tog, k6, ssk, k2. 20 sts.

Slip first 9 sts onto 1st needle, next 10 sts on 2nd needle and last st onto first needle.

Hold these 2 needles so that they form the top and bottom of the toe and graft sts together.

# BASIC INFORMATION

### Reading pattern instructions

Figures for larger sizes are given in round ( ) brackets. Where only one figure appears this means that it applies to all the sizes. Work the figures given in square [ ] brackets the number of times quoted afterwards. Where 0 appears, no stitches or rows are worked for this size.

The quantities of yarn stated in the pattern are based on the yarn amounts used by the knitter of the original garment. Yarn amounts therefore should be considered approximate as a slight variation in tension can make the difference between using fewer or more balls or hanks than that stated. My patterns quote the actual finished chest measurements of the garment after sewing up, but the schematics show the measurements of the pieces before sewing up.

### Tension

Tension is one of the most important aspects of hand knitting. The tension is the number of stitches and rows per inch that should be obtained using the same yarn, needles and stitch as the pattern requires and will always be quoted at the beginning of a knitting pattern. A variation of stitches and rows over a certain measurement can make the difference between a smaller or larger garment than the size that you are knitting, or a tighter fabric that is stiff and uncomfortable to wear, or a looser one that is unstable and stretches. A garment has been designed with the proportions very much in mind, so if you have a different stitch tension giving a wider or narrower width, but the length of the design is worked in measurement rather than rows, you will have a different shape garment to the original design.

Always make a tension square before you start the garment. Knit a sample, approximately 13cm square, using the needles, yarn, and stitch quoted in the tension note in the pattern. Smooth out the finished square on a flat surface and leave it to relax for a while. To check the stitch tension, place a tape measure horizontally on the sample and mark 10cm out with pins. Count the number of stitches within the pins. To check the row tension, place the tape measure vertically and mark out 10cm with pins. Count the rows within the pins. If the number of stitches and rows is greater than that quoted it means your tension is tighter and you need to use larger needles to create bigger stitches. If there are fewer stitches and rows, try a smaller needle to make smaller stitches. If you are only able to obtain either the correct stitch or row tension, it is the stitch tension that is the most important to get right as often patterns are calculated in measurement rather than rows.

### Care of garments

Always check the label for washing instructions. Most of the yarns used in this book are machine washable, though if possible I always prefer to hand-wash handknits. Before washing, make a note of the measurements, then after washing, dry the garment flat on a towel, patting it back into the shape if excess moisture is making it stretch slightly. Take care not to wring or rub the fabric and do not be tempted to dry it quickly with direct heat such as a radiator.

# yarn information

Do check dye lot numbers when you are buying your yarn. Yarns are dyed in batches, and the color can vary between lots. Buy an extra ball if you sometimes use more balls than the number quoted in a pattern: if you go back to your retailer later to buy extra, you may find that the same dye lot is no longer available and there will be a variation in the shade, which although you can't see it in the ball, really shows up when the yarn is knitted.

When buying yarn, always try to buy the yarn that I have used in the pattern, as I will have designed the garment specifically with that yarn in mind. It may be because a particular yarn—for example, a cotton—shows up a subtle stitch such as seed stitch beautifully, and this will be lost when substituted with an inferior yarn, or it may be that the drape is an important element of the design. However, if you do decide to use a substitute yarn, always choose the same fibre content and make sure that you can obtain the same tension. Check the meterage on the ball band; if there are fewer metres in the ball than the original yarn you may need to buy extra balls.

The following information is a description of the yarns I have used in this book and a guide to their weight and metreage.

**Debbie Bliss baby cashmerino**

55% merino wool, 33% microfibre, and 12% cashmere. A lightweight yarn, between a standard 4ply and double knitting weight. Approximately 124m/50g balls.

**Debbie Bliss cashmerino dk**

55% merino wool, 33% microfibre, and 12% cashmere. A double knitting weight. Approximately 110m/50g balls.

**Debbie Bliss cashmerino aran**

55% merino wool, 33% microfibre, and 12% cashmere. An Aran weight. Approximately 90m/50g balls.

**Debbie Bliss cathay**

50% cotton, 35% viscose microfibre, 15% silk. A double knitting weight. Approximately 90m/50g balls.

**Debbie Bliss cotton dk**

100% cotton. Slightly thicker than a standard double knitting weight. Approximately 84m/50g balls.

**Debbie Bliss extra fine merino dk**

100% extra fine merino wool. A double knitting weight. Approximately 105m/50g balls.

**Debbie Bliss alpaca silk aran**

80% Alpaca, 20% silk. An Aran weight. Approximately 65m/50g balls.

**Debbie Bliss Pure Cashmere**

100% cashmere. An Aran weight. Approximately 45m/25g hanks.

# distributors

For suppliers of Debbie Bliss yarns please contact:

## UK
Designer Yarns Ltd
Units 8-10 Newbridge Industrial Estate
Pitt Street, Keighley
W. Yorkshire BD21 4PQ
Tel: 44 (0)1535 664222
Fax: 44 (0)1535 664333
www.designeryarns.uk.com
e-mail: david@designeryarns.uk.com

## USA
Knitting Fever Inc.
315 Bayview Avenue
Amityville
NY 11701
Tel: 1 (516) 546-3600
Fax 1 (516) 546-6871
www.knittingfever.com

## CANADA
Diamond Yarns Ltd
155 Martin Ross Avenue Unit 3
Toronto
Ontario M3J 2L9
Tel: 1 (416) 736-6111
Fax: 1 (416) 736-6112
www.diamondyarn.com

## DENMARK
Fancy Knit
Hovedvejen 71
8586 Oerum Djurs
Tel: (45) 59 4621 89
e-mail: roenneburg@mail.dk

## MEXICO
Estambres Crochet SA de CV
Aaron Saenz 1891-7
Col. Santa Maria
Monterrey
N.L. 64650
Tel: (52) 81 8335 3870
e-mail: abremer@redmundial.com.mx

## BELGIUM/HOLLAND
Pavan
Meerlaanstraat 73
9860 Balegem (Oostrezele)
Tel: 32 (0) 9 221 85 94
Fax 32 (0) 9 221 56 62
e-mail: pavan@pandora.be

## ICELAND
Storkurinn
Langavegi 59
101 Reykjavík
Tel: 354 551 8258
Fax: 354 562 8252

## GERMANY/AUSTRIA/SWITZERLAND
Designer Yarns
Handelsagentur Klaus Koch
Sachsstrasse 30
D-50259 Pulheim-Brauweiler
Tel: 49 (0) 2234 205453
Fax: 49 (0) 2234 205456
www.designeryarns.de
e-mail: kk@designeryarns.de

## FRANCE
Elle Tricote
8 Rue du Coq, La Petite France
67000 Strasbourg
Tel: 33 (0) 388 230313
Fax: 33 (0) 388 230169
www.elletricote.com

## SPAIN
Oyambre
Pau Claris 145
08009 Barcelona
Tel: 34 934 87 2672
Fax: 34 678 70 8614
e-mail: marian@oyambreonline.com

## SWEDEN/NORWAY
Hamilton Design
Storgatan 14
SE-64730 Mariefred
Tel: 46 (0) 159 12006
Fax: 46 (0) 159 21805
www.hamiltondesign.biz

**AUSTRALIA**

Prestige Yarns Pty Ltd

P O Box 39

Bulli NSW 2516

Tel: 61 02 4285 6669

www.prestigeyarns.com

e-mail: info@prestigeyarns.com

**FINLAND**

Vilmiinan Villapouti

Näsilinnankatu 23

33210 Tampere

Tel/Fax: 358 (0)3 2129676

e-mail: info@villapouti.net

**JAPAN**

Hobbyra Hobbyre

5-23-37 Higashi-Ohi

Shinagawa-ku

Tokyo 140-0011

Tel: (81) 3 3472 1104

Fax: (81) 3 3472 1196

For more information on my other books and
yarns, please visit:

www.debbieblissonline.com

# picture index

BOAT SWEATER  page 10

GUERNSEY SWEATER  page 22

STRIPED HAT  page 38

JACKET WITH RIBBED YOKE

page 52

HOODED GUERNSEY  page 14

STRIPED CARDIGAN  page 28

PATCHWORK ARAN JACKET

page 40

SUN HAT  page 56

BABY JACKET WITH RIBBED

SLEEVES  page 18

JACKET WITH PATTERNED YOKE

page 32

BABY'S BALLERINA TOP  page 48

RIB AND CABLE CARDIGAN

page 58

CRICKET SWEATER  page 62

A-LINE JACKET  page 76

ZIPPED JACKET  page 92

CABLED COAT page 106

FAIR ISLE CARDIGAN  page 68

CABLE AND RIB SWEATER

page 84

FAIR ISLE BEANIE  page 98

ARAN BAG  page 112

SKINNY RIB CARDIGAN  page 72

CABLE AND BOBBLE SCARF &

MOSS STITCH BERET  pages 88/90

MOSS STITCH JACKET & MITTS

page 100

LACE SOCKS  page 116

# acknowledgements

**Acknowledgements**

This book would not have been possible without the invaluable collaboration of the following:

Rosy Tucker, for pattern checking and creative contribution.

Stella Smith, for checking and providing the schematics.

Penny Hill, for pattern compiling and organising knitters.

Tim Young for his beautiful photography, and his assistants, José, Kiri, and Marie.

Mia Pejcinovic for the lovely styling.

Kate Haxell, for being a great editor and Elvis for being a great dog.

Katie Cowan for making this book happen and Michelle Lo at Collins & Brown.

Louise Leffler for the great book design.

The brilliant knitters who work to impossible deadlines: Brenda Bostock, Cynthia Brent, Jill Borley,

Pat Church, Jacqui Dunt, Penny Hill, Shirley Kennet, Maisie Lawrence, and Frances Wallace.

The fantastic models: Alara, Brandon, Brooke, Caitlin, Cemile, Chris Badoo, Chris Gibson, Jack, Katie,

Kerry, Nell, Nicole, Rebecca, and Thomas.

My wonderful agent, Heather Jeeves.

The knitters, retailers and distributors who support my yarns and books.